JESUS
drives
me
crazy!

Resources by Leonard Sweet

Learn about these resources at
www.zondervan.com/author/sweetl

lose your mind, find your soul

JESUS
drives
me
crazy!

leonard
sweet

GRAND RAPIDS, MICHIGAN 49530 USA

We want to hear from you. Please send your comments about this book to us in care of zreview@zondervan.com. Thank you.

ZONDERVAN™

Jesus Drives Me Crazy!
Copyright © 2003 by Leonard I. Sweet

Requests for information should be addressed to:
Zondervan, *Grand Rapids, Michigan 49530*

Library of Congress Cataloging-in-Publication Data

Sweet, Leonard I.
    Jesus drives me crazy! : lose your mind, find your soul / Leonard
Sweet—1st ed.
      p. cm.
    Includes bibliographical references and index.
      ISBN 0-310-23224-4
    1. Spiritual life—Christianity. I. Title.
BV4501.3.S94 2003
248.4—dc21

                                          2003003992

Interior design by Beth Shagene

Printed in the United States of America

03 04 05 06 07 08 09 /❖ DC/ 10 9 8 7 6 5 4 3 2 1

For
Egil Waterman Sweet
Who never forgets to invite me
to "come over"

๑

Contents

Acknowledgments

The idea of the book was first presented publicly at Woodman Valley Chapel in Colorado Springs, where the talented worship team introduced me to the Nicole Nordman song "Fool for You." While I have played much music for NUTS while writing this book (Blessid Union of Souls' "I Wanna Be There," Jessica Andrews' "That's Who I Am," Keith Green's "Your Face Is All I Seek," Lenny LeBlanc's "Rainbow Song"), it's the "Fool for You" song that has danced the most with the tapping of my keyboard.

One of my online courses at Drew University helped me see that "crazy wisdom" was another, more postmodern way of talking about "excellence." The asynchronous chats among these colleagues (David E. Benson, Lark C. Brown, Bart A. Fletcher, Pamela H. Ford, Keith E. Griswold, Corey G. Miller, Steven G. Redmond, Frank Jeske, and Daren I. Flinck) and our synchronous CU-SeeMe sessions helped me become a better student of NUTS wisdom.

I wrote this book before I read two resources I wish had been available to me from the beginning. The first is Jon Spayde's "The Way of the Wacko: Rediscovering Ancient Wisdom in Which the Truth Is Nothing Less Than Crazy," *Utne Reader*, May–June 2002, 64–71 (*www.utne.com/crazywisdom*). The second is Michael Frost's *Jesus the Fool* (Sydney: Albatross Books, 1994), which I only discovered while reading a review copy of his wonderful *The Shaping of Things to Come* (Peabody: Hendrickson, 2002), co-written with Alan Hirsch. *Jesus the Fool* was a book way ahead of its time. Many bookstores refused to stock it. Some reviewers denounced it as blasphemy. Like Frost, I needed to write this book, although whether I should have written it and listened to the "don't bother people" voices is another matter. I confess this would have been a much better book if Frost and Spayde had gotten under my skin.

Two graduate students at Drew University, Chris Anderson and Andy Tyler, tracked down many of the obscure books and articles I requested without ever resorting to the Laurel and Hardy refrain of "another fine mess you've gotten me into." Joe Myers tutored me in the biblical image of the rainbow, and just when I was about to abandon the "crazy wisdom" metaphor, Chris Hughes backstopped this word "crazy," a word that too easily gives up its severity to become facile.

6

Lyn Stuntebeck protected stray days and spare moments on my calendar as well as injecting natural buoyancy into my floundering spirit. Landrum Leavell III gave the manuscript his customary naïve gaze and trained eye.

The bibliographic work for this book occurred during multiple eye surgeries for my research assistant, Betty O'Brien, who never complained about any of my e-mail "packages" even though many of them must have been about as welcome as a wrapped drum under the Christmas tree. My wife, Elizabeth Rennie, enabled me to keep heavy-lifting the luggage of language amidst life's enigmatic scribblings and scramblings, not to mention the household refrain of "Are There Nuts in the House?"

6

I dedicate this book to my youngest son, Egil Waterman Sweet. His presence in my life cannot be better described than in my version of Luke 1:78: "The loving kindness of the heart of our God who visits us like the dawn from on high." Thank you, Egil, for the "dawn from on high" you bring to and bring out in me.

NUTS Wisdom

Man's insanity is heaven's sense; and wandering from all mortal reason, man comes at last to that celestial thought.
—Novelist Herman Melville[1]

Warehouse 242 is a faith community in Charlotte, North Carolina. Its mission is to reach those who live and move and have false being, those the church usually names "lost," "unsaved," "pre-Christian," "seeker," "unbeliever," "unchurched," "worldly," "unconverted"—or more blatantly, "pagan," "heathen," "infidel." Except Warehouse 242, being aware of the way power works through language and taking a cue from the recovery movement, prefers to call those for whom their church exists the "normal" people.[2]

There is a world and wisdom according to normal. There is a world and wisdom according to Jesus. The world according to normal is the world that is. The wisdom of the world is "normal." People who don't know who Jesus is are the "normal people." People for whom God is, to quote Edwin Muir, "three angry letters in a book"[3] are the normal people.

Jesus' followers are the abnormal ones.

Disciples of Jesus are deviations from the norm. They mess up the world as it is, drawing outside the lines, thinking outside the box, resisting off-the-shelf solutions. Christians simply can't "do normal." Once you become a disciple of Jesus, normal isn't good enough anymore. Christians are part of the wisdom of the world that is to come.

In his recent book *An Hour before Daylight*, former President Jimmy Carter reflects on his childhood in rural Georgia, his relationship with his parents, and his infamous brother Billy. He writes, "Mama always said that Billy was the smartest of her children, and none of us argued with her."

> When the international news media moved into our town during the 1976 presidential campaign, Billy became the center of attention. He drank more, talked more, and saw his deliberately outrageous statements quoted as serious comments. . . . He was always good for a delightful quote. When one of the reporters remarked that Billy was a little strange, he replied: "Look, my Mama was a seventy-year-old Peace Corps volunteer in India, one of my sisters goes all over the world as a holy-roller preacher, my oldest sister spends half her time on a Harley-Davidson motorcycle, and my brother thinks he's going to be President of the United States. Which one of our family do *you* think is normal?"[4]

Christians don't see the world as the world sees itself. Christians have an off-kilter, offbeat view of the world. Like everyone else, we may see things dimly, but we also see things differently. In a postmodern world that rejects metanarratives, disciples of Jesus live by the Christ metanarrative.[5]

The number one problem of the church today? It's numbing normality.

It is not enough to say that Jesus redefined what it means to be "normal." Everything Jesus taught goes against how

Jesus Drives Me *Crazy!*

"normal" people see and function in the world. Turning the other cheek, going the second mile, giving the spare coat, washing underlings' feet, heaping blessings on those who curse you, living without anger, laying down your life—all these things "normal" people have a hard time understanding, much less thinking and living.

The truth is, Jesus stood "normal" wisdom on its head. Christians are called to see the world through Jesus' eyes, not from a normal point of view.[6] How do Christians see others—especially "normals" who are mean and hard-hearted, motivated by greed and self-gratification? Do we see them as reprobates and potential failures, or potential images of Christ who need to find their true selves?

If the only thing Jesus had given us was his signature sermon, "The Beatitudes," it would flip our world upside down the way a Sunday school teacher did philosopher Thomas Morris when he was three years old:

> My first experience inside a church did not at the time seem to bode well for my ecclesial future. The memory is still vivid. Pandemonium. I'm three years old, and a very large female Sunday school teacher is holding me upside down by my ankles and shaking me as the class gathers around us, shouting and shrieking. I'm choking on a forbidden piece of hard candy, unable to breathe, and she is determined to shake it out of me. After a good deal of jostling and back whacking, it pops free. Breathing again, I'm restored to the upright position, and the crowd of onlookers is dispersed. In many ways, this little episode inside the Westwood Baptist Church of Durham, North Carolina, is a metaphor for the role of the Christian faith in a number of my more mature struggles, even without the expected observation that has on occasion turned my little world upside down.[7]

Jesus' Beatitudes are not the only vocabulary of aberrance. Whether we're looking at the "story mode" of the gospels or the "doctrine mode" of Paul, Christianity invites us to live an intuitively counterintuitive life. There can be no "logic of faith" for a faith that doesn't abide by the logics of philosophy.

The Lifted Up One, the One who sits high and walks low, taught that the thoroughfare to God is full of bypaths and back roads.

The way up is down.[8]

The way in is out.

The way first is last.

The way of success is service.

The way of attainment is relinquishment.

The way of strength is weakness.

The way of security is vulnerability.

The way of protection is forgiveness (even seventy times seven).

The way of life is the way of death—death to self, society, family.

Know your strengths. Why? Because that's the only way you can Lay Them Down![9]

God's power is made perfect ... where? In our weakness.

Want to get the most? Go to where the least is.

Want to be free? Give complete control to God.[10]

Want to become great? Become least.

Want to discover yourself? Forget your self.

Want honor? "Honor yourself with humility."[11]

Want to "get even" with enemies? Bless and love them.

For Jesus, it wasn't enough to turn the other cheek. One had to turn the hands and feet as well in doing good to that person. Friedrich Nietzsche said such love for enemies is an ethic for cowards, deserving of contempt, not respect.

To a world obsessed with power, the gospel is nuts.

To a world obsessed with success, Jesus' teaching is nuts.

The Fox and the Hen

Barbara Brown Taylor notes Jesus' contrast between Herod "the fox" and himself as "the hen." Jesus

> likened himself to a brooding hen, whose chief purpose in life is to protect her young, with nothing much in the way of a beak and nothing at all in the way of talons. About all she can do is fluff herself up and sit on her chicks. She can also put herself between them and the fox, as ill equipped as she is. At the very least, she can hope that she satisfies his appetite so that he leaves her babies alone. How do you like that image of God?

The contrast is severe, Taylor notes: "Jesus has disciples. Herod has soldiers. Jesus serves. Herod rules. Jesus prays for his enemies. Herod kills his. In a contest between a fox and a chicken, whom would you bet on?"[12]

Nietzsche was right. To a people clawing their way to reach the top of their dungheap, this *is* nuts. The gospel presents crazy ways of thinking about power, crazy definitions of success, crazy ideas and images of the meaning and purpose of life, crazy story-lines that no author would plot.

> *When you innovate, you've got to be prepared for everyone telling you you're nuts.*
> Oracle CEO
> Larry Ellison[13]

Picture the very Son of God, sent to Earth, born of a prince and princess under a dazzling white dome with the cleanest of linen, attended by the three greatest physicians in the land, and presented to the King wrapped in a royal-blue, gold-embroidered baby bathrobe with a specially composed trumpet voluntary blaring in the background, and selected representatives from the entire realm partying outside the window and cheering, "Glory to God in the Highest."

If I told you what really happened, you'd think I was nuts.

Picture "God with us," Emmanuel, who "came not to be served but to serve," who came not to be ministered unto but to minister—with towel and basin?[14]

What kind of madness is this? A definition of leadership that turns leadership upside down? This is nuts!

A "God within" us?[15]

No wonder they called those passionate about the accessibility of the transcendent "Enthusiasts" and incurably insane.[16]

Jesus was history's biggest deviation from normal standards of being—wholly human, wholly God.[17] The predominant response to his message? Not "what wondrous love is this" but "what monstrous love is this." Jesus "came to what was his own,"[18] but his "own," even his own family, rejected him. Jesus' understanding of "messiahship" was so nuts that even those who knew him the best and loved him the most deemed it in everyone's best interests to put him away.

- What "Good Shepherd" would risk the survival of 99 safe sheep to find the one sheep that was lost?
- What father would out-prodigal his own prodigal son by lavishly giving "all I have" to his two kids in celebration of the one son's return home?
- What employer would pay last-minute workers the same wage as those who had worked hard the full day?
- What bank would reward investors who risked their clients' money in the futures market while chastizing those investors who played it safe, took no risks, but protected the money entrusted to them?
- What guest would wait until the end of a party to surprise the hosts with 180 gallons of the finest wine they would ever taste?
- What teacher would save the day by feeding five thousand listeners, only to make 12 extra full baskets?
- What aesthetics would make Jesus' greatest repulsion his greatest attraction?[19]

The Problem

The church has been in a "return to normal" mode for decades. The normalization of meaning and purpose, the normalization of what it means to be a successful human being or a "great" leader, has been pervasive partly because to do different is to be a peddler of the unpalatable.

To give more blessings than you receive?

You must be nuts!

To define success in life, not as the real estate of property, but as the *real* estate of people and relationships?

You must be nuts!

To judge ourselves, not by wealthy North American standards, but by global standards?

You must be nuts!

Once you encounter Jesus, you can never "return to normal." Authentic discipleship is an all-of-life spirituality that interrupts all of life and interprets life on God's terms. Aristides, a non-Christian, defended the Christians before Emperor Hadrian. He said of them, "They love one another, and from widows they do not turn away their esteem; and they deliver the orphan from him who treats him harshly. . . . And verily, this is a new people, and there is something divine in the midst of them."[20]

> Those who dance appear insane to those who cannot hear the music.
>
> Mark Kleiman

Here is the frightening invitation of the gospel: The more this "wild and crazy guy" (in the language of Steve Martin) Jesus is your norm, the more you become this new kind of person.

☺

Christian spirituality is anything but sane if "sane" means logical, predictable, serious, or safe. Christian spirituality is highly illogical, paradoxical, volatile, playful, and dangerous. The world of faith is freakish and unpredictable.

No wonder the more you live life on God's terms, the more the world will look on you as abnormal. The more you know the Bible, the more it's the Bible that knows you. The more status Jesus has in your life, the more you'll run up against the status quo. The more Jesus becomes the Prince of Peace, the more you'll disturb the peace. The more you give God an account of your life, the less accountants are in charge of your life. The more you keep the Sabbath, the more you'll keep your hands to the plow. The more you are charged with passion, the more you *will be charged* with passion. The more you bear thorns in your side, the more you'll be a thorn in the side of the world and the church.[21]

So: If Christians don't do "normal," what do they do? Abnormal? Paranormal? Supranormal? Exceptional?

I prefer N.U.T.S.: *N*ever *U*nderestimate *T*he *S*pirit: *NUTS.*[22] The wisdom of Jesus is a NUTS wisdom.

> **Relax! Go NUTS!**
> Planters slogan

"God helps those who help themselves." That's the World and Wisdom According to Normal.

"When we were still powerless, Christ died for the ungodly."[23] That's the World and Wisdom According to NUTS.

We "look on the outward appearance."[24] That's the World and Wisdom According to Normal.

"But the LORD looks on the heart."[25] That's the World and Wisdom According to NUTS.

"Seeing is believing." That's normal wisdom.

"Unless you believe you shall not understand."[26] That's NUTS wisdom.

> **The Trouble with Normal Is That It Always Gets Worse.**
> Songwriter Bruce Cockburn (1981)[27]

NUTS wisdom is disturbing and unsettling. Normal wisdom equates intelligence with spiritual depth. What nuttiness is this, that God would have, as Jesus said, "hidden these things" from the titled and talented and "revealed them to infants"?[28] It's often not the richest people or smartest people who live the richest and smartest lives. Intellectual giants can be spiritual pygmies, and the greatest in heaven's kingdom are those willing to play and pray on their knees and become "like children."[29]

The "normal" world is a materialistic world. After Nine-Eleven, our politicians pleaded with us to "get back to normal." What did they mean by normal? "Normal" meant shopping and traveling. It became our patriotic duty to lay out and get about: not to lay aside our "wants" and put away our "resources," but consume and spend.

> **Buying is much more American than thinking.**
> Pop artist
> Andy Warhol

The World According to Normal is a world of perishable commodities.

The World According to NUTS is a world of imperishable connections.

To break with the so-called world of normal does not mean to leave the world of normal. It does mean to release normalcy's stranglehold over the spirit, to reduce participation in worldly games. While the church is not encampments on embankments, for the church to be "in the water" means traveling salmon-style up streams rather than always going with the flow. In the words of the old gospel song, "This world is not my home, I'm just a passin' thru." Ironically, this is the ultimate "Go with the Flow" because life lived this way flows with the Spirit.

The gospel turns the world upside down and then refuses to pick up what falls out of its pockets. The biblical contrast between the ways and wisdom of the world and the ways and wisdom of God could not be clearer. "I will boast all the more gladly of my weaknesses, so that the power of Christ may dwell in me. Therefore I am content with weaknesses, insults, hardships, persecutions, and calamities for the sake of Christ; for whenever I am weak, then I am strong."[30]

> *He hung therefore on the cross deformed but his deformity is our beauty.*
>
> Augustine of Hippo (A.D. 354–430)[32]

For the NUTS disciple, "normality" is a Goldilocks world where everything seems the wrong size. Christians are a little "off." Their perceptions of truth, goodness, and beauty are "off." The very image of God's glory and beauty came in one with "no beauty or majesty."[31] Golgotha, the greatest defacement of beauty (the crucifixion), became the Mount Everest of beauty. The concept of a crucified God was deemed so offensive, so crazy that Christians were accused of madness for even suggesting the idea. That's why not until the fifth century did images of Jesus on the cross begin to appear.

6

All people are different, but some are more different than others. And Christians are the most different of all. When God pronounced the judgment against Israel through Ezekiel, it was because they "profaned my holy things."[33] The Hebrew word "profane" means to "make ordinary" or "normalize." The church has normalized God. We have judged what is a successful church by the world according to Normal, not the world according to NUTS. We have played the game of life by the rules of the world and Robert's Rules, not the rules of the Spirit.

Too much of Christianity is nice-ianity, not NUTS-ianity. Too much of the church sees the world as the world sees itself, rather than seeing the world through the eyes of faith and the Bible. Jesus never met a Christian. I wonder what he would say if he met one today. Would Jesus be a Christian today?

The Hebrew word for "profane" can also mean "wound." By "normalizing" God, we "wound" God's name and power. Normalcy is to be fought by all means at our disposal. In fact, the process of dying to normal and living to NUTS is what it means to be a "new man" or "new woman" in the language of the Scriptures.

Just as demographically there is no such thing as average anymore—no average person, no average citizen, no average Christian, not even an average Baptist or Methodist or Presbyterian—so according to the Bible there is no average or lukewarm or normal church either.

In some of the most squawky words in the Scriptures, we read, "Because you are lukewarm, and neither cold nor hot, I am about to spit you out of my mouth."[34] The word "spit" really means "vomit." In other words, God is saying to all conforming and average churches, "You make me sick!" A "normal" dose of religion is a dangerous thing. It numbs us to our real need: total transformation of heart and life. It makes God puke.

> He's always happy . . .
> NO, wait, he's
> always mad.
>
> Homer Simpson
> *(The Simpsons)*
> on God

The Challenge

Our challenge is to make NUTS the accepted (ab)normality of the church. One NUTS-normal church is Cokesbury United Methodist Church in Knoxville, Tennessee. Just before the pastor, Steve Sallee, picked me up before the first Sunday morning service, an attendant at the Best Western where I was staying asked me, "Are you here to preach at that Kooksbury Church?"

Just right.

Another name for us besides "kooks" is "fools."[35] It's hard not to talk Jesus-talk without sounding like a fool or a complete idiot. Our word *silly* today means "foolish," but in

> *But the "wisdom of God" was always "foolishness*
> *with men." No marvel, then, that the great mystery*
> *of the gospel should be now also "hid from the wise*
> *and prudent," as well as in the days of old;*
> *that it should be almost universally denied,*
> *ridiculed, and exploded, as mere frenzy,*
> *and that all who dare avow it still,*
> *are branded with the names of*
> *madmen and enthusiasts!*
>
> Charles Wesley[36]

Middle English it carried the sense of "simple" or "innocent" *(sely)*. Even more revealing are its roots in the Old English *saelig*, which meant "happy" or "blessed."[37] Fools are people possessed, even blessed. In ancient traditions there was a tendency to regard the insane as "God touched"—"s/he's touched"—off-center, even addled.

Christians had better be "touched." And it had better be more than a temporary insanity. Christians are holy fools, possessed by God and blessed by the divine "touch" that has left us as "touched" as Jacob's wrestling with an angel left him limping. If clowns are "professional fools," Christians are full-time, dedicated fools.

The apostle Paul, who himself admitted that "I have been a fool,"[38] made a consistent case for the ways of Jesus being the ways of a fool: "If you think that you are wise in this age, you should become fools so that you may become wise. For the wisdom of this world is foolishness with God."[39] A few paragraphs later, Paul elaborates the underlying reason behind fooldom: "We have become a spectacle to the world, to angels and to mortals. We are fools for the sake of

Jesus Drives Me Crazy!

Christ."[40] Or, in what amounts to a Manifesto for Fools, Paul's fullest explication of the NUTS doctrine:

> But God chose what is foolish in the world to shame the wise; God chose what is weak in the world to shame the strong; God chose what is low and despised in the world, things that are not, to reduce to nothing the things that are, so that no one might boast in the presence of God.[41]

⑥

This image of the church as jester to the world has specific historical meaning. Kings of old would keep jesters close by to provide them with reality checks and to poke out their folly. Andrew Stark points out that Beatrice K. Otto's study of court jesters shows how

> when a jester wanted to lampoon a monarch's intellectual foibles, he wouldn't simply show off his own superior intellect—that would have made him a pedant, not a fool—but rather he would make use of a kind of moral authority. Consider Birbal, jester to the sixteenth-century Indian Emperor Akbar, who used a moral argument—more specifically, a straight-faced attempt to carry out the monarch's own moral code—to show up Akbar's intellectual lapses.[42]

The story as Otto tells it is that

> Akbar had a prize parrot that he valued above all his other pets. He warned his servants that they must look after it well, for whoever brought him the news of the parrot's death would himself have to die. Despite their best efforts the parrot died, and they were too frightened to tell Akbar, so they appealed to Birbal. Birbal went to him to tell him how amazing the bird was, since it had reached a state of perfect *samadhi* and was a real yogi. The king wanted to see this for himself and was enraged when he saw the dead parrot: "The bird isn't in *samadhi*, you fool! He's dead." The royal trickster smiled, "Your Highness must die, according to your own decree, for telling you that the

parrot is dead." The king had no choice but to admit his folly—"I sometimes say foolish things"—and to laugh the humorous laughter which is directed at oneself, and in that laughter forgive his servants, his jester, and himself as well.[43]

But there is a deeper level of meaning to Paul's "fool" passages than exegetes have customarily seen. The Greek word Paul routinely uses is *moros*. Scholars have chosen to translate *moros* as "fool." But *moros* equally means insane, crazy, mad, nuts.[44] Paul is really saying here, "I'm nuts." Could Paul be inviting the church here to "go nuts"?

CRAZY in Church

There are problems with the metaphor of NUTS. A student who read an early draft of this summarized them in the following fashion:

I do not like this term. I was raised to be orderly in church. There is too much mental illness in my family for me to relate to "crazy" as positive and all right. I also come from stoic Swedish ancestors who do not "go wild." I have yet to serve a church who goes wild for anything and certainly not Jesus.

Yet, I think this CRAZY is what I am missing in church. No one is excited about Jesus. No one is excited about church. I remember when I was a young Christian, I was so excited. I wanted to preach; I wanted to tell everyone how great Jesus is. The pastor's wife told me the best place for new Christians was in a closet, because new Christians turn off more people than they convert. I never liked that description. There are many days now that I wish I had half of the enthusiasm I had back then. I never doubted God's existence. I expected prayers to be answered. I knew God cared for me and loved me. I knew God had a plan for me and all I had to do was find it and fit in. I really was CRAZY for Jesus at one time.

Now I am an Elder in the United Methodist Church. I am tired and I do not want any trouble in my church. I do not want the D.S. [District Superintendent] coming in to set anyone straight. No one is CRAZY in my church.

Jesus wants to drive you crazy. In fact, the fundamental identity of a NUTS disciple is this: Someone who is crazy in love ... with God, with life, with the world. There is nothing that makes you more passionate, more obsessed, or more crazed than being in love. We can't love God first. God first loved us.[45] But NUTS disciples are lunatics for love—the first to love others.

Why does this sound haywire? Because popular culture has used this metaphor of "crazy" to help normal people bring life to a boil. I grew up listening to the salty sweetness of Patsy Kline's "Crazy." Paul Simon's "Still Crazy after All These Years" is a testimony I want sung at my funeral (if it can be said honestly). My kids introduced me to the Aerosmith song "Crazy," and though I try hard to rid my ears of the ringing, I can still hear Brittany Spears sing "(You Drive Me) Crazy."

Christians are people who let Jesus drive them crazy—"crazy" in the sense that they no longer aspire to normalcy. A disciple (or better yet "apprentice," says philosopher Dallas Willard) is someone who is crazy in love with Jesus because Jesus is crazy in love with them.[47]

The aim of discipleship is a love relationship with God and life. Judas stopped being a disciple, not when he betrayed Jesus, but when he fell out of love with him. Judas, like many of us, less loved Jesus than he loved himself in Jesus. Jesus, the NUTS wisdom-master, couldn't help himself from loving others, even those who didn't love him back.

> *O eternal, infinite God! O mad lover!*
> *And you have need of your creature? It seems so*
> *to me, for you act as if you could not live*
> *without her, in spite of the fact that you are*
> *Life itself, and everything has life from you*
> *and nothing can have life without you.*
> *Why then are you so mad? Because you have*
> *fallen in love with what you have made? . . .*
> *You clothed yourself in our humanity, and*
> *nearer than that you could not have come.*
>
> Catherine of Siena[48]

The officials of a railroad, disturbed because commuters neglected to close doors in winter weather, put up signs that read, "For the comfort of other passengers, please close the doors." The doors stayed open. The poster was changed to read, "Please close the doors for your own comfort." The doors were closed.

This story helps me understand why one of the best-selling stickers sold at the Universal Studios complex in California reads, "It's all about me," or why the number-one magazine in South Africa is entitled "YOU." Our true Latin slogan is less *E Pluribus Unum* (out of many one) than *Pro Se Quisque* (every person for himself/herself).

NUTS wisdom says it's not all about me. And it's not all about you, either. "It's all about *you,* Lord," as the praise chorus says. The gospel is *not* just about you. The cross is not a big plus sign for your life. God didn't send Jesus to please *you;* God sent Jesus to help you please God. Normal people define the "good life" in self-gratifying ways. NUTS

Jesus Drives Me Crazy!

people define the "good life" in God-pleasing ways. When the apostle Paul lifted the trapdoor of his soul's stage, he revealed this behind-the-scenes truth: "I have not come as a great philosopher; I did not come for great arguments. The only thing I have to offer is Christ Jesus."[49]

"NUTS" may mean "off" or even "off the wall," but it is not to be confused with "off the trolley." There are people with "misplaced marbles," people who are genuinely "nuts" and belong in an "acorn academy" or "squirrel tank."

It may be psychiatrists who get to decide who is "nuts" and who is "sane" in the "normal" world. But not in the NUTS world. What is normal and what is exceptional is God's determination.

You can have all your marbles, but still be NUTS.

Ask yourself, "Am I NUTS?"

Ask your church, "Are there NUTS in the house?"

Ask your friends, "Anyone for NUTS?"

Frederick Buechner, one of the few clergy ever to pull off well the hat trick of becoming at once priest and novelist, is a virtuoso word-smith. My favorite quote in the vast corpus of his writings is a cut to the theological chase. I have even given the quote a pet name: "Jesus 730":[50]

> The reasonable man adapts himself to the world: the unreasonable one persists in trying to adapt the world to himself. Therefore all progress depends on the unreasonable man.
>
> George Bernard Shaw in *Man and Superman*

If the world is sane, then Jesus is mad as a hatter and the Last Supper is the Mad Tea Party. The world says, Mind your own business, and Jesus says, There is no such thing as your own business. The world says, Follow the wisest course and be a success, and Jesus says, Follow me and be crucified. The world says, Drive carefully—the life you save may be your own—and Jesus says, Whoever would save his life will lose it, and whoever loses his life for my sake will find it. The world says, Law and Order, and Jesus says, Love. The world says, Get, and Jesus says, Give. In terms of the world's sanity, Jesus is crazy as a coot, and anybody who thinks he can follow him without being a little crazy too is laboring less under a cross than under a delusion.[51]

Too much is made of mental health anyway. To be a disciple of Jesus is hardly to have a smoothly rounded character. How many biblical characters can you name who were balanced of mind? Since when have spiritual masters lived "balanced" and "orderly" lives? Since when did divine revelation come in neat and tidy packages or unambiguous glimpses? Since when were creativity and mental disorders unrelated?[52] "The lunatic, the lover, and the poet," Shakespeare wrote, "Are of imagination all compact."[53] To name the names of Robert Schumann, Frederic Chopin, James Joyce, August Strindberg, John Keats, Lord Byron, Herman Melville, and Henry James is to name mental instability and incomparable genius.[54] I tease my therapist friends with Karl Kraus's contention that "Psychoanalysis is that mental illness for which it regards itself as a therapy." The goal of psychotherapy is to return you to "normal." The goal of Christian spirituality is to drive you NUTS.

Sociologists Samuel and Pearl Oliner have co-authored a study comparing those who helped rescue Jews from the Nazis and those who ducked for cover. Called *The Altruistic Personality*, their book claims to have discovered four key differences that separated the 406 "rescuers" who got involved at the risk of their own lives from the 72 "bystanders"

who stood there and did nothing.[55] Of the four key contributors to an "altruistic personality," this one stood out: Rescuers had home lives where spirituality was a defining component. In the case of Christians, these "rescuers" exhibited an extreme form of faith. "They were Christians with a capital C."[56]

Jesus never tolerated small-"c" mediocrity in the life of faith. Since when did the gospels portray Jesus' followers (or Jesus himself) as "balanced"? Where did we get this notion that a consecrated life is head-centered, left-brained, right-wing, even-tempered, danger-free? One of my favorite characters in church history is Margaret Fell, George Fox's right hand in the formation of the Society of Friends.[57] Fell and Fox were labeled "Quakers" because of their "shriekings, shakings, quakings, roarings, yellings, howlings, tremblings in the bowels, and risings in the bellies" (as described in a 1655 pamphlet). Or, as Ronald Rolheiser puts it, "Given that God is fire, . . . isn't it the task of the Holy Spirit to introduce some madness and intoxication into the world? Why this propensity for balance and safety since . . . don't we all long for just one moment of raw risk, one moment of divine madness?"[58]

> *A leader is a fellow who refuses to be crazy the way everybody else is crazy and tries to be crazy in his own crazy way.*
> Peter Maurin[59]

Look at all those in the Scripture of whom it can be said, as Barney Fife said of Ernest T. Bass, "He's a nut, a real nut." Would any of the disciples have gotten past boards of ordained ministry or screening committees? Two of the most unlikely NUTS were Peter and Paul. One had an "anger" problem; the other, an "authority" problem. Peter the fisherman—impetuous, impulsive, stubborn, loquacious, defying. Paul the tentmaker—merciless, zealous, persecutory, bureaucratic, obedient. Some of the greatest saints were high-octane sinners and holy lunatics.

But our Nutcracker God has a way of prying open our nuttiness and releasing God's Spirit.

Moses stuttered.

David's ego was bigger than his armor.

John Mark was rejected by Paul.

Hosea married a prostitute.

Amos thought fig-tree pruning was a homiletics class.

Jacob was a liar.

David had an affair.

Solomon was too rich.

Abraham was too old.

David was too young.

Timothy had ulcers.

Peter was afraid of death.

Lazarus was dead.

John Mark was naked.

Jesus liked to hang around with trouble-makers and troubled people.

Naomi was a widow.

Isaiah had a branded tongue.

Jesus heard voices.

Paul saw visions.

Jonah ran from unwelcome voices.

Miriam was the voice of gossip.

Gideon and Thomas both doubted.

Jeremiah was depressed, suicidal, and always crying.

Elijah was burned out and liked to run around naked.

John the Baptist was a loudmouth who lived on locusts.

Martha was a worry-wart and subject to anxiety attacks.

Mary was lazy.

Samson had long hair and was short on self-control.

Noah got skunk drunk.

Did I mention that Moses had a short fuse?

So did Peter and Paul, who feuded with one another publicly.

I could keep going.[60]

A NUTS disciple represents an otherness that can be frighteningly subversive. NUTS people do things that aren't safe, aren't predictable, aren't normal.

But when God drives you NUTS, God drives you divine.

> *Sometimes you feel like a NUT.*
> *Sometimes you don't.*
>
> Slogan of Almond Joy/Mounds Bars

⊚

The essence of a NUTS discipleship that can turn the world right-side up is found in the profound simplicity of four words: *Be There With All*. The talismanic quality of these four less-is-more words becomes more apparent with every passing prayer.

> *We generally find it easier to understand what is complex; what is simple is too demanding.*
>
> Theologian Hans Urs von Balthasar

These four simple words are enough to fill a life. They are enough to live day by day. They are enough to die for at any moment. Master these four words, Be There With All, and your discipleship will be righteous, your church will become a commons where normies can gather, and your life will be transformed into an incarnational, relational nutscape overnight. Plus, you'll drive the world crazy.

part 1

Incarnational Discipleship
BE THERE

*Know the enemy and know yourself; in
a hundred battles you will never be in peril.
When you are ignorant of the enemy but
know yourself, your chances of winning
or losing are equal. If ignorant of both your
enemy and of yourself, you are certain in
every battle to be in peril.*

—Sun-Tzu, *The Art of War*[1]

In Tina Sinatra's biography of her father, Frank Sinatra, she pays the Chairman of the Board the ultimate tribute. Her dad was "like a campfire, the point where we gathered and felt warm. He had such a big presence. . . . When he was with you he was really *with* you."[2]

What's the greatest compliment anyone can receive? "Thanks for . . . being there."

What's the greatest condemnation anyone can make against you? "You were never there!"

What's the greatest promise anyone can make to another person?

At one point in my ministry, when I was president of United Theological Seminary in Dayton, Ohio, I confided to my best friend, gardener/nonagenarian Marie Aull, that I didn't know whether I could continue in that role but that if I quit I didn't know what I would do.

> With an adorable, never-ceasing energy, God mixed Himself up with all the history of creation.
>
> John Henry Newman

She encouraged me to continue, not to get discouraged in well doing. But the most important thing she said to me was this: No matter what you decide to do, Leonard, I will be there for you—no matter what!

The greatest promise anyone can give you? "I'll be there."

These two little words—"Be There"—define the essence of the greatest thing that has happened in history since the creation of the universe—the incarnation.

The centerpiece Christian doctrine in the Eastern Orthodox tradition is the incarnation, which the Orthodox believe is the greatest artistic creation in the history of the universe. If it is true that we are living "at a time of almost unparalleled theological stress in which the positive formulation of the substance of the Christian faith (rather than its merely negative criticism) is a pressing necessity,"[3] then it is time for the Western church to remove the incarnation from the periphery and place it where it belongs—under the central spotlight of theology. It is also time to take up once again the symbol of the incarnation—the cross, eternity's intersection where the human and divine come together to create a new center for the universe.

It was the contribution of neo-Platonists to conceive of God as above and beyond particularity. It was the contribution of Judaism to conceive of God as one who loved all creatures and wanted a relationship with them. It was the singular contribution of Christianity to conceive of a God who subjected the very divine being to the limitations of particularity and humanity. The enduring appeal of my favorite devotional poet is George Herbert's masterful ability to put this "scandal of particularity" into verse form. He is rightly called "the supreme English poet of the Incarnation."[4]

> *Jesus didn't submerge Himself in a cloistered Christianity as we do. He mixed easily. From the wedding feast at Cana to Matthew's dinner party, Jesus ate with rip-off-artist tax collectors and low-life sinners, earning a reputation as "a glutton and a drunkard" (Luke 7:34). Like Him, we need to be missionaries, becoming acquainted with the undesirable portions of our culture.*
>
> Jan Johnson[5]

The essence of the incarnation is irradiating the human with the divine. In Latino terms, the incarnation is the quintessential *mestizaje*, the juncture of humanity and divinity. God wants to turn normal people NUTS. How? "The life that he once lived on earth, he lives again in me." We have been "ingodded"[6] by the divine to the point where matter bears the holy and the mortal bears witness to the eternal. "The moment I consider Christ and myself as two," Martin Luther liked to say, "I am gone." Or as St. Bernard put the essence of little incarnations four centuries earlier, "I and Jesus have one heart."

"Be There" is the essence of NUTS discipleship.

"Be" refers to character. "There" refers to context. "Be" is face. "There" is place. To "Be There" is to know your face ("Who am I? What am I here for?") and know your place ("Where am I? What is to be done?"). To "Be There" is to get your act together and get other people together: to know Christ and to make Christ known. The Christian life is the process of becoming who we are in the moments we have been given.[7]

It is in the interaction between the inner and the outer, the character of Christ and the context of culture, that the identity of Christianity consists. NUTS discipleship exhibits this double loyalty—true both to one's unique identity as a disciple of Christ and at the same time true to one's unique cultural context. Every incarnation is heavily dated,[8] and no ministry should be "out of date."

> *Now my eyes will be open and my ears attentive to the prayers offered in this place. I have chosen and consecrated this temple so that my Name may be there forever. My eyes and my heart will always be there.*
>
> Yahweh[9]

No church has an intrinsic right to exist. It is not enough for a local church simply to be there on the corner without "being there." A church's "right" to exist is earned by the price it is willing to pay for these two words: Be There.

"You're a Known Nutcase": BE

The face is the soul of the body.
—Ludwig Wittgenstein

Do you know who you are? Are you clear about who you are? Do you know why you're here, what is the mission of your life? "Be" is the mastery of character. Only if you stand strong in the strength of who you are can you let others be who they are and you be free to accept others as they are.

I hail from mountain culture. My father was born in the foothills of the Adirondack Mountains of New York, and my mother was born in the Allegheny Mountains of West Virginia. Part of being a product of the mountains is bracing each fall for the tourists—"leaf peepers" we call them—whose annual rite of lifting up their eyes unto the hills to see the autumnal fireworks was as humorous to us "homies" as it was essential to our economic survival.

As mountain people know, leaves don't really turn colors in the fall. As the days grow shorter and the temperature drops, the trees stop manufacturing chlorophyl, which covers up the "true colors" (or carotenoids) of the leaves—bashful yellows, show-off golds, boastful oranges, hide-and-seek russets.

NUTS disciples with character let their true colors show. When the chlorophyl of conventions and civilities and compromises and contingencies and coded conduct no longer is pumping, what shows? When the long, green summer drops its veil, what is revealed?

What are your "true colors"?

Face Value

People can "read" the grammar of your face. There is a reason people equate your "self" with your "face." Most of the nonverbal messages we transmit are through the face. The human body can produce up to 700,000 distinct physical signs. There are more than 1000 different bodily postures, and more than 5000 hand gestures—and more than 250,000 facial expressions.[10]

> Not everything that is faced can be changed,
> but nothing can be changed until it is faced.
>
> Novelist James Baldwin[11]

Philosopher Jean-Paul Sartre once proposed in all seriousness that human beings create their own faces. Three features of a baby's face suggested to Sartre that we are born without a face.

First, whatever proud parents may say, "all babies look very much alike."

Second, "a baby's face tells little about the personality of that child. Looking at a baby's face gives you little indication as to what kind of character that person possesses and will develop."

Third, beauty in a baby's face is "almost totally genetic." Whether a baby is good-looking or not depends almost entirely on its "genetic endowment."

This is true for a baby when it is first born. But this changes with each hour, day, and year of its life. According to Sartre, the process culminates at age forty when, at last, life has carved the essential lines of a face. "At that age, we look different from anyone else in the world (even if we have an identical twin), our face speaks volumes about who we are, and our physical beauty has begun to blend with our general beauty." We are now judged to be good-looking, or not, on the basis of who we are more than on the simple basis of our physical endowment. After age forty, our faces reveal individuality, character, and a "beauty-beyond-genes."[12]

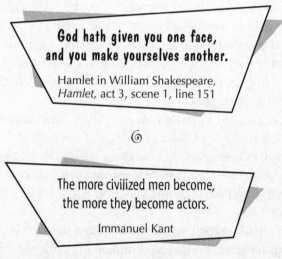

God hath given you one face, and you make yourselves another.

Hamlet in William Shakespeare, *Hamlet,* act 3, scene 1, line 151

The more civilized men become, the more they become actors.

Immanuel Kant

Without strong roots, our faces can quickly become farces. "The first duty in life is to be as artificial as possible," Oscar Wilde wrote sarcastically. "What the second duty is no one has yet discovered."[13] Jesus spent his entire ministry unlocking one prison after another. And he never used the same key. Each of us is locked in artificial cages forged with one-of-a-kind hammers and heat.

> And I will pour out my Spirit and my blessings on your children. They shall thrive like watered grass, like willows on a river bank.
>
> Isaiah[14]

The apostle Paul warned, "Do not let the world squeeze you into its mold."[15] That word *world* could be crossed out and *church* or *family* inserted without distorting Paul's forewarning of life's fossilizing forces. There is a variety of ways one can "run with the pack." There are numerous ways of turning normal. One way of losing our spiritual senses and turning normal is in herd-thinking, the ultimate in mass madness. The conformism of the church scene and its repression of "alternative" ways of being a Christian can be a real show-stopper. The church opposes biological cloning but practices spiritual cloning with particular relish and finesse. Since when did personality-bypasses become the specialty of the Great Physician? Do we really think the same God who created a gallimaufry of species and an arkful of odd specimens expects us all to act, look, think, and worship alike? Might not quirks of personality actually suggest quarks of genius?

God created each one of our faces an original. God made each of us a classic. Life's biggest question is this: Will you have enough class to become a classic, the classic God made you? Will you live inside your own life, or will you look on from the sidelines? Will you allow God to be God in you?

An eighth-grade English teacher liked to inject big words into his lectures, hoping to stimulate his students' curiosity about their meaning. Responding to the challenge, a student interrupted a lecture to ask the teacher to explain the meaning of the word *phenomenon* he had just used. The teacher explained as follows:

If you see a spiny cactus plant, that is *not* a phenomenon. If you see a bird that sings, that is *not* a phenomenon. If you see a cow, that is *not* a phenomenon. But if you see a cow sitting on a spiny cactus plant and singing like a bird, that *is* a phenomenon.

Each person God created is a phenomenon, an original, one-of-kind, nutso—a cow sitting on a spiny cactus plant singing like a bird. Whereas history's tyrants and terrorists teach "no one is indispensable" (one of Stalin's favorite sayings), Jesus taught that every single "you" is infinitely precious, hugely valuable. You're not like anyone else who has ever been or ever will be. It's not enough to say, "You're one in a million." If that's so, there are 6000 others out there right now just like you.[16] The truth is, there has only ever been, and only ever will be, one you.

Whatever happened to all the geniuses grandparents talked about? If genius is innate brilliance, great originality, and diehard determination, then every child is a genius.

What happens to us? We're not wearing our true face.

Our lives get chloroformed by the chlorophyl of convention and swamped by "normality." The search for "true colors" and the "real self" is the source of some of the world's greatest literature and music. Do you know your nuts-y story? Do you know how to tell your story? Even better, do you know how to live your story, how to sing your song?

One of my favorite pastors/composers/praise and worship leaders, Joseph Garlington, from Pittsburgh, asks us to repeat these words to ourselves: "Jesus has some strange kids."

> **Folks may say you're different, that you have gone and lost your senses, but the world is yours to walk in, go ahead and leap the fences.**
>
> *Sesame Street*

You may be tempted to mutter under your breath so I can't hear you, "And I'm glad I'm not one of them," but it is my duty to tell you, "Yes, you are." . . .

God is out to reconcile all things to Himself in Heaven and in earth. When I first came to Christ, I had some hang-ups.

As I continued to walk with Him, I still had some hang-ups. I have to admit that as I write these words, I still have a few hang-ups. (If you ask [my wife] Barbara, she might expand or expound on my statement, so don't ask her.) Somebody said it like this: "He was hung up for my hang-ups." Aren't we all glad for that? We need to understand that *it really was God* in Christ reconciling the world to Himself and that it is God in you who is reconciling the world to Himself. People need to be able to come up to you and say, "I rejoice in the Christ that is in you."[17]

Poet/engraver William Blake, who in a despairing hour complained, "O why was I born with a different face?"[18] went on in another work to answer his own question:

The apple tree never asks the beech how he shall grow: nor the lion, the horse, how he shall take his prey. . . . The eagle never lost so much time as when he submitted to learn of the crow.[19]

Ever since the moment Adam and Eve tried to hide their nakedness and scars from God and covered themselves, we have been covering ourselves. We humans have been in the "makeup" mode for our faces, with some faces so heavily made up the face is effaced along with the blemishes. Ever notice how some people, when you meet them, appear to have no face? Either they look like a thousand other people, or they are so nondescript you look right through them.

Character is destiny.
Greek philosopher
Heraclitus

The greatest personal statement you will ever make is not your words. It's your face. You get the face you desire. You get the face you deserve. Sometimes, someday, your face gets set. "What a beautiful soul this person has." Or, "that person's soul lies behind a face that is as starched as his collars."

Your soul is showing.

What's the soul showing on the faces of our churches?

Face-Lifts

Many of us, and many of our churches, may need a face-lift. The more our furrowed brows look down on others, the more our character is in need of a face-lift. In fact, as Fleming Rutledge reminds us, "bad characters are the only kind of characters God has to work with; there are X marks over against everybody in one column or another."[20] The basic constitution of the character of a Christian is not all goodness. None of us has reason to boast. Yet none of us is too bad a character to be redeemable by a face-lift. God entrusted the Ten Commandmetns to a murderer. As that first Christian in heaven (the thief on the cross) reminds us, there is nothing you can do that is so bad that God's grace can't overcome it.

Perhaps we need to hear two stories from normal people reading our faces.

Story number one: She could never quite force herself into a church building. She could be seen every Sunday, waiting outside the church door, sitting on the steps, peering into the faces of those who filed into and later emerged from the building. She eventually wrote down her reason for not going in:

> I looked at their faces. I saw their faces preoccupied with anxiety and self-preoccupation—faces not unlike my own. If only I could have found *one* face which reflected any new light as a result of that religious exercise, I surely would have rushed into the church, excitedly, and flung myself before the altar. But no, not one, not a clue that a seed had grown, a ray of light had burst, and a note had sounded.

Story number two: Some years ago a Christian journal carried the lament of a woman who, with some bitterness, explained why she did not believe in God. Never in her explanation did she mention dogma, morals, or church authority. For her, the credibility of God and of Christ depended more on something else, the faces of Christians. Her complaint went something like this:

> "Don't come talk to me of God, come to my door with religious pamphlets, or ask me whether I'm saved. Hell holds no threat more agonizing that the harsh reality of my own life. I swear to you that the fires of hell seem more inviting than the bone-deep cold of my own life. And don't talk to me of church. What does the church know of my despair—barricaded behind its stained-glass windows against the likes of me? I once sought repentance and community within your walls, but I saw your God reflected in your faces as you turned away from the likes of me. Forgiveness was never given me. The healing love that I sought was carefully hoarded, reserved for your own kind. So be gone from me and speak no more of God. I've seen your God made manifest in you and he is a God without compassion. . . . I shall remain an unbeliever."[21]

One reason so many of our faces look as if following Jesus is more a life sentence than a lifestyle is that we're trying to wear someone else's face instead of our own. I have seen some of the most beautiful people in the world with the ugliest faces, and some of the ugliest people in the world with the most beautiful faces. No wonder a whole industry has arisen to deal with the problem of "I'm not myself." This feeling of being "not myself" is the number one cause of depression, the most common mental disorder of our time, the ailment of the modern world.[22]

> *There's no art
> To find the mind's construction in the face.*
>
> Duncan in William Shakespeare,
> *Macbeth*, act 2, scene 4,
> lines 11–12

Ask the Mask

One meaning of "iconoclasm" is to make a face unidentifiable. We are God's icon. For us to mask or make up or disfigure our face is the divine version of "iconoclasm."

The association with face and mask is endemic. The very word *person* comes from the Greek *persona,* which means a mask worn by an actor on stage. Then the word *person* came to mean our interface with society and, later, the character of the mask-wearer ("personality"). Today *person* means "self."

Too much of the "self" is a fake face. There is a variety of ways to mask our face. Historian Michel Foucault said that he wrote "in order to have no face,"[23] sheltering his private, reclusive self in an avalanche of verbiage and friendliness.

But all masks ultimately fall. All masks *must* fall— at least if NUTS are to emerge. You can't get to the nut without cracking the shell.

What masks the face of God in us? The big one, of course, is "sin." In the words of Isaiah, "Your sins have hidden his face from you."[24] Postmodern philosophy contends that all thought is an attempt by those in power to impose their will on others—a restating of the basic biblical insight that unredeemed humans are self-centered to the point of making war against our own weakest members.

But anything that takes the place of God masks God's face. It can be religion itself. Or it can be rules and regulations and rubrics, which especially became our sacred objects in the modern world.

Or it can be our fear to wear the face God gave us (that is, be the "character" God made us) that masks the face of God in us. Jungian psychologist James Hillman notes that every person has a unique vocation or character. This "character," he writes, "is not what you do, it's the way you do it."[25] For sociologist and political theorist Richard Sennett, "character" is the capacity to make and keep commitments—in every arena of one's social life—and the ability to provide continuous, coherent narratives of personal experience.[26]

To say that the twelve disciples were a cast of characters would not begin to do justice to the reality. When did it happen that to call someone a "real character" became a form of character assassination? When did it become a crime to be different? How many people would be complimented being called "a character"? We are afraid of being called the best thing anyone could ever call us: a "character."

That's because too many disciples today are lightly character-ized. We have plastic morals to fit a plastic society. Hence the laments "You're better than that" or "That's out of character for you." Character-ized discipleship—that is, true discipleship based on "character," discipleship that has NUTS "characteristics," discipleship that is rooted in NUTS wisdom ideals, integrity, and identity—wears an original, one-of-a-kind face. The familiar NUTS text from John 3:8 ("You do not know where it comes from or where it goes. So it is with everyone who is born of the Spirit.") is not about the unpredictability and singularity of disciples of Jesus who are filled with the Spirit.

> *To be nobody-but-yourself—in a world which is doing its best, night and day, to make you everybody else—means to fight the hardest battle which any human being can fight; and never stop fighting.*
>
> Poet e. e. cummings[27]

Face-to-Face

The only face disciples of Jesus are to wear other than our own is the face of Christ. Our "be-ings" are shaped by all sorts of things. In Western culture we most often construct our self, our being, from the consuming culture. Buying an identity—"the commodity self"—is what most people mean by the word *style*. In many ways, our "be-ings" are a compilation of our favorite brands and bands.

In contrast, the Christian "be-ing" is formed, reformed, and transformed by the character of Christ. There is a new theory about why newborn babies stare into their mother's face. The mother's face may be the mirror that infant needs to create a sense of self. Newborn children can start recognizing facial expressions as soon as 42 minutes after birth. Around the mother's look the infant constructs a reality, a universe of sentiments and sounds that become its character. Without a parent's look of love, there is disfigurement.

This is the way it works when newborn Christians stare into Jesus' face. We are assembling a character, as Jesus imprints our face with a true self. Just as Jesus "set his face" toward Jerusalem, we must "set our face" toward Christ. Spiritual formation is really Christ-formation: "My dear children, for whom I am again in the pains of childbirth *until Christ is formed in you*."[28] And again: "We proclaim him, . . . so that we may present everyone *perfect [complete] in Christ*."[29] Automorphosis is self-transformation of the self. Theomorphosis is God-transformation of the self.

Every NUTS disciple has gone in for a Jesus face-lift. A fourth-century writing called the *Acts of Pilate* tells the story of a woman who was so anxious to see Jesus as he carried his cross up the Via Dolorosa that she pushed her way to the front to the crowd. When she gazed on his face, she was so moved that she wiped his bloody face with her veil, which thereafter bore the imprint of his features. The name of this woman—Veronica—only gets into the story in a twelfth-century British retelling of it by the chronicler Gerald of Wales, who points out the obvious: Veronica comes from *vera icon* ... "true image."[30]

Each of us is called to become a true image of Christ, to become a Jesus face. In this new kind of being we are given, Jesus frees us from ourselves. And when we are free from having to find our own "identity" and discover our "being" in Christ, we truly become "free" to be ourselves.

Have you ceased living for yourself? Are you living for the One who for your sake died and was raised to life?

Perhaps we could learn some things from Lee Strasberg's "method acting" regimen, which has shaped the art of people like Paul Newman, Anne Bancroft, Montgomery Clift, Jane Fonda, and Marlon Brando. In method acting you don't so much "play a role" as "inhabit the character's life." You don't "imitate" a character but "live" and "become" that character. In method acting you take on the character of the person you're playing.

NUTS disciples "take on" the character of Christ. In the psychoanalytic community, "transference" is bad.[31] In the community of the church, "transference" is how disciples of Jesus can live most fully and completely. As we "take on" the likeness of Christ, his attitudes and attributes get "transferred" to us. Aristotle noted long ago that humans acquire attributes by acting in certain ways. "We become just by performing just actions," he wrote, "temperate by performing temperate actions, brave by performing brave actions."

In the same way, we become NUTS by performing nutty actions.

This is Christian maturity: the transference of Christ's character by the power of the Holy Spirit. That is why godly character is "the fruit of the Spirit."

I never did like the phrase "imitations of Christ." I don't have it in me to imitate the Son of God. I can't even imitate the sons and daughters of greatness. I'm not even going to try to be a Monet or a Mozart or a Georgia O'Keefe "wannabee." But what if Monet could paint his picture through me? What if O'Keefe could use my life as her brush? What if Jesus were to live his life through me? What if my life could become an instrument in God's hands—a "pencil in God's hands," as Mother Teresa once put it, writing a "love letter to the world"?

NUTS wisdom is not "imitation" of Christ. NUTS wisdom is participation in Christ. NUTS wisdom is implantation with Christ. Of course, the highest form of NUTS discipleship is incarnation.

Katie von Bora, the "woman who house-broke Martin Luther," said on her deathbed, "I will stick to Christ as a burr to a topcoat."[32] The disciple Philip said, "Lord, show us the Father." Jesus answered: "Whoever has seen me has seen the Father."[33] That's why I hang on every word Jesus spoke, every thing he did, every place he went. That's why, like Katie Luther, "I will stick to Christ as a burr to a topcoat."

NUTS disciples don't put on a happy face. Nor do they put on a proper face. They put on a Jesus face.

Is there such a thing as a typical, or composite, Christian face? Are there some inherent and immutable character traits of a Christian? Wouldn't a "Christian face" be one lined with emotions and intelligence, a little naive but mysterious, not too refined or urbane, not at all grumpy, a lot of depth showing with cheerfulness creeping in every crevice, wrinkle, and blink?[34] Simply facing a Christian Face should increase the joy of living on earth.

There is something absolutely grace-full that takes place when our be-ing takes on the being of the divine and our face the face of Christ. In the sacred writings of Judaism we learn that after Esau received him, his brother Jacob testified of the encounter, "to see your face is like seeing the face of God."[35] After Moses' encounter with God on Mount Sinai, his face shone so brilliantly that the Israelites could only give his face fleeting glances.[36]

Paul's first glimpse of God was so dazzling it blinded him. The transfiguration had Jesus' face shining like the sun, and as Jesus prayed, "the appearance of his face changed."[37] The glory of God shines through Jesus' face,[38] although the fullness of that glory will only be apparent at the second coming, since now we see with glimpse and glaze but one day with gaze and glare, even "face to face."[39] Fourth-century Gregory of Nyssa's "bold request" which reached the very top of "the mountains of desire" was this: "to be filled with the very stamp of the archetype . . . to enjoy the Beauty not in mirrors and reflections, but face to face."[40]

Is your face shining? Whose face are you wearing? A face that has been shined on by God? NUTS people are those with holy sparks flying all around them.

Lose Your Mind

To put on the mind of Christ, you have to lose your mind. But in losing your mind, you come to your senses.

The more we become like Christ,
   the more we put on the mind of Christ,
      the more we morph into the face the Christ,
         the more unique our faces become.

When God gets big in each of us, when Christ is on the increase, we don't disappear but appear as we were meant to be.

When our face is being transformed into the face of Christ, we all look different. That's because the face of Jesus looks different to every person. In the same way each one of us looks different to every person who sees us, Christ's face looks different depending on your angle.

The poor person who comes to know Christ sees in him riches that remove the pain of poverty. The rich person who comes to know Christ sees in him a generosity that frees him from the prison of greed and selfishness. The depressed person who comes to know Christ sees in him a hope that lifts life from the depths.

Each of these—the poor, the rich, the depressed—reflect the face of Christ that they originally imitated. What is more, the face takes on other wrinkles and dimples (even what we may consider blemishes) that reflect other aspects of Christ in intersection with their lives.[41]

Christian "be-ing" is not an abandoning of identity but a turning toward God and an indwelling by God that enhances our identity and uniquity. You become more *you*, more unique, and more original the more you become like Christ. Jesus shows us what we did not know we were. When you let the truth become itself in you, you let you become yourself in you. The more "I belong to Christ" and "I belong to you," the more "I belong to me."

> **The work of the Holy Spirit does not create standardization. It unleashes the divine potential in every human being.**
> Mosaic pastor/author Erwin McManus

To be sure, character is transformed by action. Character is not infused in us magically by the Spirit. It takes practice and discipline. It takes habits that become habitations. These spiritual practices are the genuine growth-rings that expand and build the tree of character.

Live the Mystery

I can't seem to get out of the book of Colossians in general, and this one verse in particular: "The mystery . . . has now been revealed . . . Christ in you, the hope of glory."[42] Maybe the reason I'm stuck here is the same reason that 18th-century evangelist George Whitefield couldn't stop preaching on the text "Ye must be born again." When people asked Whitefield why he preached so often on this one passage, he replied, "Because, Ye must be born again!"

Life is the living of The Mystery. As one Greek Orthodox theologian put it, "We see that it is not the task of Christianity to provide easy answers to every question, but to make us progressively aware of a *mystery*. God is not so much the object of our knowledge as the cause of our *wonder*."[43] What are doctrines but vestibules to the mysteries? To follow Jesus is not a paint-by-numbers path. To follow Jesus is to live the adventure and experience the mystery of faith.

When we become "stewards of the mysteries," we enter a world inhabited by angels and visions, a world swathed in mystery and magic.

In the eucharistic liturgy, the significance of one phrase easily slips by: "Let us proclaim the mystery of faith: Christ has died, Christ has risen, Christ will come again." There are two parts to the declaration of that mystery that "Christ will come again."

First, Christ comes again in each of us. The virgin birth takes place in each one of us. That is why I have never been comfortable giving up that "born-again" language. The incarnation is not something that just happened once.

> *At bottom every man knows well enough that he is a unique being, only once on this earth; and by no extraordinary chance will such a marvelously picturesque piece of diversity in unity as he is, ever be put together a second time.*
>
> Friedrich Nietzsche

The incarnation is something that must happen in each one of us if we are not to be only half born. It is not enough to hear the angels say, "For *unto* you is born a Savior, Jesus Christ the Lord." The character of a Christian is to hear, "For *in* you is born a Savior, Jesus Christ the Lord."

"What does God do all day?" asked 13th-century mystic Meister Eckhart. "God lies on a maternity bed giving birth." God calls each one of us to be a Mary: to give birth, to make flesh of God, to birth Jesus in us and for our world. The mystery of God's birth wants to happen in you. Becoming a character is the incarnational process of giving birth and body to the divine. If novelist Italo Calvino is right that "the aim that all of us should have must be that 'the writer and reader become one, or One,'"[44] how much more should the aim of discipleship be that the disciple and Master become one, or One?

> **God's everlasting birth.**
> Theologian Martin Buber

> *Let your own "being you" sink into and flow into God's "being God."*
>
> Mystic Meister Eckhart[45]

Excelsis Smith had a most obstreperous small niece. Whenever he fell heir to the task of baby-sitting her, his wits were taxed to the utmost answering her questions and inventing ways to keep her unrelenting mind entertained.

One Sunday morning he had taken her to church, thinking the hymns and Scripture passages and sermon would keep her thought processes occupied without his help for an hour. But the respite was short. She emerged from the church full of questions.

"The sermon was on the Holy Spirit," she began. "What is this Holy Spirit?"

"Well," he said, "the Holy Spirit is a person, a part of the Trinity."

"I know all that, but what does He do?"

"Well, He lives within each Christian, helping him to live as a follower of Christ."

"Are you a Christian?"

"Yes."

"Then do you have the Holy Spirit in you?"

She had caught him off guard.

"Well, I . . . what do you mean, do I have the Holy Spirit in me? Do you mean, can I feel Him in me?"

"No, I just mean do you have the Holy Spirit in you?"

"Well . . . I . . ."

"If you are a Christian," she went on, "and Christians have the Holy Spirit living in them, then you must have the Holy Spirit in you. Right?"

"Well . . ."

"That must be a wonderful thing," she said, "to actually have the Holy Spirit living in you."[46]

The first part to the declaration of the mystery of faith is that Christ comes again in each of us.

The second part is that Christ comes again by calling each and every one of us into ministry and mission. Karl Barth says that our calling to ministry "is in its own manner and in its own place no less than the Christmas mystery of the birth of the eternal Word of God in the flesh." The call to ministry is an impregnation of our life with the Spirit of God until we give birth to the Word of God in us. Each minister has been born, "not of blood or of the will of flesh or of the will of man, but of God."[47]

> **Christ has no body now but yours.**
> From a prayer of Teresa of Ávila

Revelation is more than an event or a set of propositions. Revelation is an ongoing participation in the life of Christ. Jesus is not a Product That Works. Jesus is not an Absolute Principle. Jesus is a Person who is Real and Active in our world, a Divine Presence that is True and Indwelling. Truth is never about things or principles. Truth is always about relationships and revelations. How did God choose to reference the infinite in the finite? Is the grammar of the Holy Spirit propositional semantics? The truth of God is larger than creeds and confessions, rubrics and rituals. Belief is based on certainty. Faith is based on trust in the midst of uncertainty.

Truth is trust.

Did Jesus come to deliver us some teachings? Or, did Jesus come to reveal to us the character of God? The point of Christianity is not a point. The point is a person.[48] The point of Christianity is not believing a doctrine but experiencing a reality that transcends all concepts and categories. That's why the very attempt to talk about theological mysteries using philosophical categories, according to Martin Luther, is akin to trying to put "new wine into old wineskins."[49] The faith and practice of the church is Christ. The apostle Paul wrote, "All the treasures of wisdom and knowledge" are hidden in Christ.[50] Have you found them? Are you looking for them?

Maybe you can't teach Christianity. Maybe you can only incarnate Christianity by taking on the character of the Infallible, Inerrant Word-Made-Flesh-and-Dwells-Among-Us Image of God. In what is undoubtedly the most amazing thing Oscar Wilde ever wrote: "Jesus Christ does not come into the world to teach one anything, but by being brought into his presence one becomes something. And everybody is predestined in his presence. Once at least in his life each person walks with Christ to Emmaus."[51]

Do you believe this?

Then you're NUTS!

The ultimate task in life is "to be" and "to arrive at being." It's the ultimate art form: the artistry of being.

"In a Nutshell": THERE

People get ready
there's a train a-coming
you don't need no baggage
you just get on board
—Singer Curtis Mayfield

The nuttiness of incarnation is that God sanctifies each cultural "there" as a site for the divine birth. Christianity began as a breakaway Jewish movement in the Eastern Mediterranean. But the earliest Jewish disciples experienced a Jesus who opened up their faith to culture-specific ways of being a Christian (context) while retaining a constitutive identity and integrity (character). The apostles didn't insist that Greek Christians copy the lifestyle of observant Jews and their way of being a Christian. They encouraged Greek disciples to find Greek ways of being a Christian, of opening up Greek life to the Jesus experience, and, beyond Hellenistic culture, of inviting people of every culture to turn their own way of life toward Christ. This is the secret of how Christianity became geographically global so fast: the face of Christ showed different features in every context.

The essence of the incarnation is the gospel's ability under the direction of the Holy Spirit to throw on and off the garments of its age, cross ethnic frontiers, and become culturally at home throughout history and geography. Starting in Antioch (Acts 11), Jewish disciples began to encourage Gentiles to make sense of Jesus in non-Jewish terms. Will moderns insist that Jesus make sense only in modern terms? Or will moderns permit Jesus to make sense in postmodern terms?

The full "fleshing out" of the body of Christ is the embodiment of the gospel in every cultural setting, which is the Great Commission.[1] The body of Christ is sedimentary, less in the geological sense of being built layer upon layer of cultural and historical incarnations ("sedimentation") and more in the fluvial sense of the river that is being constituted by the dynamic movement of the current, which builds up its banks and carves out its contours by the ever moving flow ("sediment").[2] It takes all the cultures of the world to build up the body of Christ. Attaining "the full stature of Christ" depends on bringing all the body parts together.[3] To "make the river flow" fully, all the tributaries of the world need to make their sedimentary contributions.

NUTS disciples (remember? Never Underestimate The Spirit) are those who grow their character in the context of which they are a part.[4] "Contextualization," the key word in missions circles for over two decades, can be defined as the cultural expression and extension of incarnation. To contextualize the gospel is to bring the character of Christ into conversation with the local cultures of humankind. It is another way of talking about Paul's desire to become all things to all people in order to turn some from the rocks against which humanity dashes itself towards the Rock on which humanity is saved.[5] If you're preaching in Ephesus, you'd better take seriously the goddess Artemis (Diana).[6] If you're preaching in New York City, you'd better take seriously the gods of that city, such as materialism, consumerism, fashion, and relativism. If you're a cultural icon like Bono, you'd better use pop culture to critique and condemn its obsessions, as U2 did on the CD *Pop* (1997).[7] All ministry is contextual because all ministry is cross-cultural.

In the novel *Bee Season* by Myla Goldberg, young Miriam Grossman, like other members of the Naumann family, is on a quest for wholeness. One day, while she is still peering into a kaleidoscope in a playback scene, someone rotates it. In that momentary jerk, Miriam discovers a new understanding of perfection: a perfection that movement doesn't destroy, but creates anew.[8] In the same way, every turn of the clock brings a fresh opportunity for us to create incarnation anew.

There is no one who is not trapped in time. One day we will take on the trappings of eternity, but until then we must be true to our context and time, knowing that our children will need to be true to theirs as well. Something can be very much of its time and place and yet stand the test of time. In fact, it is only when we enter time that we can be taken out of time.

Right after the movie *Armageddon* came out in 1988, a story circulated about what would happen if planet Earth were given advance notice that a tsunami was about to hit in ten days. A New York rabbi had an interesting response. He said,

> I think the religious leaders of this city would take over. In New York City, for example, masses and other devotional services would be 24/7 at St. Patrick's Cathedral. The Billy Graham Team would conduct round-the-clock prayer services at Madison Square Garden. The mainline Protestants would have their best preachers conducting marathon preaching services at Riverside Church. And New York's leading rabbi would assemble the Jewish population and address them in these words: "Ladies and Gentlemen, we now have ten days in which to learn how to live underwater."

The rabbi got it. Learning to live underwater, if that's where you must live, is the essence of the incarnation.

The worst state to be in—at least for a church touched by God's incarnational love—is a church out of touch with its culture. One of the most damning things for a historian to say of any religious leader is "he was out of touch with his times" or "she missed her moment." Why would the church want to make that condemnation into a compliment? NUTS disciples aren't cultural absenteeists or abstentionists. The Spirit drives us to be in touch with the culture. Always in tune with the Spirit, but in touch with the culture. NUTS disciples don't stand apart from culture and then reach down (depending on which level of Dante's hell you're in) with ice tongs or asbestos gloves to pick it up.

NUTS disciples live their context and love their context. Jesus' demanding challenge of being "in/not-of/but-not-out-of" the world cannot be met once and for all time. It is subject to continuous renegotiation and rendition. NUTS disciples know the microclimate of the weather patterns (intellectual, social, political, scientific) in which they live, not with the goal of Christ transforming culture but with the goal of the Christ who transcends culture transforming persons and communities in every culture. To "Be There" is to live simultaneously as an insider and an outsider.

Much of the church today is resisting its divine "placement." In fact, the church today is failing to pay attention to its "place," so much so that it is possible to speak of the church's "there" psychosis.

The world has changed.
Opening line of movie
Lord of the Rings: The Fellowship of the Ring (2001)

A "there" psychosis is worse than denial. Denial is not taking your medicine. Some studies put the figure as high as 50% of patients who don't take the medications their doctors prescribe. A goodly number don't even bother to fill their prescriptions. The medical world

Christic and Culture

I write this after the 50th anniversary of the publication of H. Richard Niebuhr's *Christ and Culture* (1951). There is a desperate need for a new treatment of this topic that is intimated in the following quote from Peter Slater:

> The history of missions teaches us that Christianity cannot be separated from culture and that each specific culture needs to be transformed, including that of the earliest and most established churches. Peter's Judaic Christianity was transformed by Paul's more inclusive vision. Eternal Rome hosted Vatican II. These facts reinforce the point that the presence of Christ in each worshiping community is never completely realized. The whole Christ cannot be reduced to what we know locally of Jesus in Jerusalem or anywhere else. No culture is so perfect as to embody fully the Spirit of the living Christ. If everything local were to be considered divinely sanctioned, the Gospel would be buried in the culture. There is thus much to be rejected as well as much to be transformed. The local here includes Victorian England, the Kaiser's Germany, Orthodox Russia, Lincoln's United States, and the Italian Curia, as well as Benares, Mount Fuji, and Mecca.
>
> The process of becoming Christ-like calls for listening sometimes to the Christ against culture, for instance, that of apartheid, and sometimes of the Christ *of* culture, for instance, that which we find in great art or music. The process overall, however, is of Christ transforming culture. The guidelines include not only the sense of what Tillich named the "Catholic substance" and "Protestant principle," but also the principle of creative justice that vindicates the crucified in the renewed community. It is the risen Christ who is said to be known in the breaking of the bread and whose Spirit is present when two or three gather in his name. In brief, the Holy Spirit is said to act sacramentally, speak prophetically, and move us all eschatologically toward universal reconciliation.[9]

calls this "noncompliance," which poses, one official says, "a huge problem larger than anyone imagines."[10]

A "there" psychosis is different from bad timing. Samuel T. Lloyd III, rector of Trinity Church in Boston, invited a consultant to lead a staff retreat. "I've discovered," the consultant said, "that I'm not very good at telling time." She went on to explain what she meant by this. Everything in life has its own pace and timing—people, groups, places, institutions. "And often," she said, "I can't tell whether this is the beginning of something that needs to emerge, or it is late in something and it is time for it to end. But I know I need to get a feel for the timing." The church's timing is so bad, so "off," that its "feel for the timing" is borderline neurotic.

A "there" psychosis is different from a "there" neurosis. The difference between a neurotic and a psychotic? Psychotics actually believe 2 + 2 = 5. Neurotics know 2 + 2 = 4 but don't like it. When in denial, truth gets put into the back of the mind.[11] You don't want to face it, or when you do face it, it's untimely. Denial is neurotic. When you're in psychosis, you actually convince yourself that something is true that isn't.

> *You can wake someone who's sleeping. But you can't wake someone who's pretending to be asleep.*
>
> Old Indian saying of villagers in the Narmada valley

What do psychotics do? They impose their fancies and fantasies on others. They persuade themselves that Julia Roberts really loves them or that John Lennon wants to kill them or that something is true that really isn't. Or, in the case of a "there" psychosis, that it's not really a different world out there and that the world we feel most comfortable in is the world we're really living in.

You tell me: Does the church have a psychotic break with reality or doesn't it? How much of the church hasn't heard that the 20th century has ended? How much of the church hasn't heard that the 19th century has ended? How much of the church still thinks the world out there is the Ollie ("another fine mess you've gotten me into") and Ozzie (and "Harriet!") world I grew up in rather than the Ozzy (and "Shaaaaron!") world that is actually out there?[12]

I used to think the church's inability to understand the rapidly changing world in which we live was neurotic. I'm now convinced it's psychotic. But our psychotic alignment with the place we're in exists alongside a neurotic interpretation about our place in the world. It's one thing for people to rest serenely in the limbo of our psychosis and never realize the ragbag of changes taking place during our lifetime. The masses of people do that. But it's another thing to call yourself a leader and not "be there." It's another thing to call yourself a preacher and conduct worship that bears no discernible trace of the world you inhabit.

The good news is that there is nothing in our genetics to predispose the church to psychosis or to keep us stuck there. Quite the opposite. NUTS disciples are charged with an EPIC[14] task: to break the psychotic break with reality, and to put the church's face, not its back, to the future.

> I hazard the prophecy that that religion will conquer which can render clear to popular understanding some eternal greatness incarnate in the passage of temporal fact.
>
> Philosopher Alfred North Whitehead[13]

If you don't think it's a new "there" out there, you ought to have your screens recalled. Tom Peters tells his corporate clients, "If you're not ready to be enterprise-and-industry-reinvention evangelists, then do yourself and everyone else a favor: Get out of your job."[15]

The biggest issues facing the church are the "there" questions, especially the here-to-there questions ("*Can* we get from here to there?" and "*How* do we get from here to there?"). "Here-to-there" conflict is the biggest growth industry in the church today.

My favorite parable of ministry is the story of a mail carrier delivering the mail. Let's say his name is Norman, and he's filling in for his friend Nancy.

Norman approaches one walkway and sees on the porch an Eskie, a little white snowball of a dog eyeing him warily from the side and growling. He's seen dogs before, and this fluffy white thing doesn't seem terribly threatening. At least he's not barking outright. So Norman goes about his business, smiles, and says, "Nice doggie."

And the dog bites him.

"I don't get it," he later grumbles to Nancy.

"You did five things wrong," Nancy explains. "First, dogs don't speak English. They speak Dog. Second, you smiled and bared your teeth. To a dog, that's a threat. Third, you probably made your eyes wide and looked straight at it. That's also a threat. Fourth, you entered its territory without slowing down or turning sideways, which escalated the conflict. You're supposed to show some fear, or at least stop if you stare back. And fifth, nothing personal, Norman, but your ears stick out. You might as well have worn a sign saying, 'BITE ME.'"[16]

Many of us in ministry are like Norman: We have the best of intentions and are working harder than ever to deliver the gospel better. But our message isn't getting across, and we're carrying scars from the bites and bruises of our efforts.

> *There is no place in the Christian world that is less prepared for the new world than the church's theological academies.*
>
> Andrew Walls, St. Andrews, Scotland

One of our problems is that we have failed to be as good at cultural exegesis as we are biblical exegesis. We are better at God-Talk than God-Walk in this new culture that is a-borning. We are failing to demonstrate ways by which God's timeless love letter can become timely—the only "special delivery" that actually delivers people from the bondage of sin and death.

There's a lot of "there" that I don't like or understand. I can push the moral panic button as hard as anyone.

As a writer, I don't like it that I'm living in a world of such cultural vulgarity that "the most powerful character in modern melodrama" is a cannibal and psychopath named Hannibal Lecter.[17]

As an academic, trained in a Gutenberg curriculum and context, the knowledge that films influence my kids more than books releases more penance than pleasure. It is somewhat mortifying to learn that there is now at Washington State University a Taco Bell Distinguished Professor of Hotel and Restaurant Administration.[18] There is now at Stanford University (no slouch school) a Yahoo! Chair with an emphasis on information systems technology.[19] The most "distinguished" professors of marketing at the universities of Arizona and West Virginia hold the Coca Cola Chair and the K-Mart Chair respectively.[20]

As a father I am horrified that television's so-called "family hour" is filled with explicit sexual material and jokes about oral sex, masturbation, pornography, and homosexuality. Fox's family-hour *Boston Public* actually showed teenagers in a school hallway engaging in oral sex.[21] I am angered by the images and antics of MTV (Music TV).[22] I am horrified that when I went to school, the press covered stories of how my coeds could cram into a phone booth; now that my kids are going to school, the press covers stories of how many men porn stars can have sex with at one time.

As a USAmerican, I am embarrassed by what Read Mercer Schuchardt calls the "complete cultural victory of pornography in America today." He says, "Hollywood releases four hundred films each year, while the pornography industry releases seven hundred movies *each month*. The domain name 'business.com' recently sold for a record-breaking $7.5 million—but in a recent court case, the domain name sex.com was valued at $65 million. Not surprising, since porn is, at a minimum, a $10 billion a year business."[23]

As a human being I am scandalized by the fact that postmoderns are more likely to be outraged by the suggestion of violence to animals than they are by the slaughter of their own kind. I have been to movies where, in the process of making the movie, actors and stunt crew were injured, maimed, and killed, yet there was the assurance at the end of the credits that "no animals have been harmed during the production of this movie." In one movie about insects, they even said, "No insects were killed during the production of this movie."

> *No ship exists*
> *to take you from yourself.*
>
> Egyptian poet Cavafy[24]

A shipwrecked mariner had spent several years on a deserted island. Then one morning he was thrilled to see a ship offshore and a smaller vessel pulling out toward him.

When the boat grounded on the beach, the officer in charge handed the marooned sailor a bundle of newspapers and told him, "With the captain's compliments. He said to read through these and let us know if you still want to be rescued."

We are living in wacko times. And the times may get even wackier. But the church's usual response to cultural innovation and change is condemnation and isolation rather than incarnation and participation. Go back two centuries ago and remember how dime novels and penny dreadfuls were no sooner evoked than evicted from church life. Ditto the theater, the music hall, the waltz, jazz, radio, television, movies, comics, rock music, computer games. Very early in *The Lord of the Rings: The Fellowship of the Ring*, Frodo says he wishes the master ring had not been found in his lifetime. "So do I," said Gandalf, "and so do all who live to see such times. But that is not for them

> *It is a common*
> *apprehension of the*
> *world that it was*
> *young when we were*
> *young, grew old with*
> *us, and is finally*
> *too far gone for us*
> *to be very upset*
> *about leaving.*
>
> British poet
> Hugo Williams

to decide. All we have to decide is what to do with the time that is given us."[25]In the movie the screenwriters use these words twice and link this quotation with another that says it is not the evildoers who are in charge. It was the dark lord Sauron, after all, who created the great rings to rule Middle Earth and the "One Ring to rule them all." In addition to asking why this ring was recovered in his time, Frodo asks why this ring found its way to Bilbo Baggins, his kindly uncle. In both the book and the movie, Gandalf replies, "Behind that there was something else at work, beyond any design of the Ring-maker. I can put it no plainer than by saying that Bilbo was *meant* to find the Ring, and *not* by its maker. In which case you were also *meant* to have it. And that may be an encouraging thought."[26]

No matter how bizarre or off-putting, NUTS disciples are those who will "be there" for the world in which God has placed them.

The number one war going on in the world at the beginning of the 21st century is between open systems and closed systems. This war is being waged in every nation, every business, every religion, and every community. Nine-Eleven was only one manifestation of the fight between a closed system and an open system.

> Today is the tomorrow that yesterday's leaders told us we could ignore.
>
> Anonymous

In fact, al Qaeda can best be seen as an allergic reaction or an immune response to open systems and systems that are becoming even more open.[27] Osama bin Laden is a closed-system evangelist.[28] His intended audience for Nine-Eleven was not so much Westerners as the 1.3 billion[29] fellow Islams he is intending to convert and rally to his brand of Islam, which aims to bring down "the infidel" and "the Great Satan" of open systems. Nine-Eleven was designed to convince the world's Muslims to return to the closed teachings of Islam. The terrorists' intent was not to inflame just USAmerica, but also Arab streets.[30]

Closed-source operating systems are those like Microsoft, which guards its "source code" as if it were Fort Knox. Open-source software such as Linux, Apache, Global Grid Forum, and Internet protocols html and http feature source codes available to all. Anyone can see the applications, modify them, and critique them without centralized controls. This open development and decentralized peer review ensures that it gets better the more people use it.[31] And more people are using it. The Linux operating system is even migrating to handheld devices.

Self-avowed open-source "evangelist" Eric S. Raymond uses the metaphor of the "cathedral" model that dominates the commercial world versus the "bazaar" model of the Linux world. The idea that software "needed to be built like cathedrals, carefully crafted by individual wizards or small bands of mages working in splendid isolation, with no beta to be released before its time" is contrasted with Linus Torvald's style of development, which is "release early and often, delegate everything you can, be open to the point of promiscuity. . . . No quiet, reverent cathedral-building here— rather, the Linux community seemed to resemble a great babbling bazaar of differing agendas and approaches."[32]

If you're thinking either-or, the open movement owns the future. The bazaar wins out over the cathedral.[33] Closed systems and other destructive orthodoxies of modernity are exhibiting the "supernova effect"—a supernova being a dying star that gets bigger and brighter in the very process of dying. Closed systems are supernovas. The flair that you see is their flare for dying.

Nine-Eleven was a fear response of a closed system to a future that looks more and more like an open-source movement. The world's first "open-source" consumer product is a soft drink called "OpenCola," which gives its recipe away on their website (www.opencola.org).[34] Current other "open-source" projects include "OpenLaw,"[35] Open-Audio,[36] and an encyclopedia called Wikipedia.[37] People are even becoming more open-source in their spirituality,[38] as fewer are drawn to closed-source systems (whether denominations or religions) and look more to open-source systems (whether nondenominational churches or create-your-own spiritualities).

Closed-source leads to re-creative versions of modernity—1.1 Christianity, 2.5 Christianity, 9.0 Christianity, xp Christianity, and so on. Open-source releases the energy of the priesthood of all believers; it is context creative and gives permission for the church to be as creative missionally and spiritually as the culture is creative technologically.

But if context is not to drive out character, the future needs both proprietary platforms and open platforms. When it comes to dominant operating systems for life, we need *both* Linux (open-source) and Windows (closed proprietary systems). Life works both bottom-up *and* top-down.

This is the NUTS wisdom of life systems: Run both an open system and a closed system. It is part of the both/and nature of the gospel.

> The laity, on the whole, have been in the stands as spectators, and the clergy have been on the field playing the game. . . .
> The laity must come out of the stands as spectators and take the field as players; and the clergymen must come off the field as players and take the sidelines as coaches of a team.
>
> Missionary/evangelist/theologian E. Stanley Jones

There is a real hunger out there for truth that is rock solid and water soluble, a faith that is not as easily moved as Peter and is as constantly in movement as Paul.[39]

Every "open" person[40] needs both openness and closure. The integrity of the self requires closure. But to get beyond the self and to care for others requires openness to others.

In the computer world this is called "double-boot," the running of both open-source software and a closed-source system simultaneously.[41] In the religious world this is called the ability to "be there"—to have an open-sourced ministry and be a people of the open movement while at the same time exhibiting loyalty to a platform, to the protocols and processes of a closed system.

Here are some key features of double-booting in the Era of the Open Platform, this open-source 21st-century world. Here is what would happen if the cathedral embraced the bazaar:

Double-Boot No. 1

Open system: face the future.
Closed system: lean back into the past.

Open System: No one can escape the future. But some people are going into the future not leaning backwards and kicking forward but facing backwards and being dragged forward. The NUTS wisdom of *epektasis* portrays the soul as stretching toward the future, or, in the Apostle Paul's poetic phrasing, "straining forward to what lies ahead."[42]

"Don't ask me about what was, but what is to come," Peter told the early Christians.[43] We need to point people in the same direction. Leaders are those who keep an ear cocked for the heartbeat of the future. My Appalachian gramma used to say she could feel the weather in her bones. Leaders can feel the future in their bones. Christian leaders circulate "thy-kingdom-come" future in their blood.

Born several years B.C., Jesus was a man ahead of his time.

The challenge of this moment in time is that the future is no longer wrapped up

> *The things we expect to happen always happen more slowly. It's the surprises that overtake us.*
>
> Futurist John Naisbitt

in stability and predictability. The future now is discontinuous, dominated by exponential growth and change, and thus risky. Did you notice how fast Nelson Mandela went from being a prisoner to being president of South Africa?

"Everything changed on Nine-Eleven" is a common refrain.[44] But it's wrong. Everything now is always changing and changing everything. The truly "new" something in the history we are living now is the exponential nature of change.[45] Philosopher Mark C. Taylor calls this "the moment of complexity."

> To understand our time, we must comprehend complexity, and to comprehend complexity, we must understand what makes this moment different from every other. What distinguishes the moment of complexity is not change as such but rather the acceleration of the rate of change.[46]

The rate of change now doubles every decade. That means that "we'll experience 100 calendar years of change in the next twenty-five years." Our kids during their lifetime will experience the change of a millennium. "The 21st century as a whole will experience almost one thousand times greater technological change alone than did the entire 20th century."[47]

The evidence is all around us. In 2001, 17,000 new grocery products were introduced, yet the average grocery store stocks only 30,000 items. The price paid by marketers for Web traffic dropped as much as 99% in a 99-day period. In five months Napster went from having 1 million to 10 million users; 11 months later it had 80 million users. It was the most successful technology introduction of all time. And then one day it went dark. Nothing. Out of business.

To ask whether impermanence and change can be our friend is another way of asking whether the future can be our friend. Sometimes God leads us out of the order of Egypt and into the chaos of wilderness. Will we just drift into the future, or will we dialog about it—argue over it, debate it, direct it? Where are the sustained, serious conversations in the church regarding the future? How many Christians have ever even heard of, much less read, the most important article yet published in the 21st century—Bill Joy's "Why the Future Doesn't Need Us"?[48]

Part of the "complexity moment" in this Information Age is the complexification of the relation between spirit and matter—or incarnation. To "be there" for the future means to incarnate the gospel through uninsured initiatives in the midst of incomplete information and constantly changing assumptions.

The business world has a phrase: "consequence management." When we fail to "carpe mañana"—seize tomorrow—and get ahead of things, we are reduced to managing consequences, not mastering conditions. In the words of one journalist covering the war in Afghanistan, "It used to be that 'having been there' was enough for a new story; now it is not enough. It is necessary to be pre-positioned—in the right place at exactly the right time."[49]

If there is any religion that should be good at this, it should be Christianity. When we lean back into our genes, we find that our ancestors have always met God when they moved forward, not backward. In what may be the most important study on eschatology in the 20th century, Jürgen Moltmann argues that God's middle name is "Future," that God speaks to us from the future and calls us to follow and move forward from the future. We worship a God for whom "the future is his essential nature."[50] In fact, Paul's future orientation defined Christians in terms of living in conformity with the future, not the past. In the words of Pauline scholar Paul J. Achtemeier, commenting on Romans 13:11–14, Christians are "creatures of the future, not the past. To it they are to look, and by it they are to act."[51]

> *The future has an ancient heart.*
>
> Old Italian saying

Closed System: The one sport I regret never entering is track and field. I dreamed of the pole vault and long jump. No pole-vaulter stands at the bar and jumps. No long-jumper stands at the sand pit and leaps forward. To jump high or long, an athlete must first go back. In fact, the momentum of going back is what propels us forward.

NUTS wisdom lives out of (not in) the past. Business futurists tell us that when paradigms change, everything goes back to zero. For disciples of Jesus, when paradigms change, everything goes back, not to zero, but to the beginning. This is the real meaning of "originality"—back to origins, to the original vision of our ancestors. The original vision of Christianity was NUTS. Jesus and his disciples made strange and unsettling claims that were mind-bending and life-transforming. What happened is that gospel's NUTS wisdom became creedalized, bureaucratized, and institutionalized. Only NUTS wisdom can return us to the original vision.

The irony of our situation is that this emerging culture is much more first century than 20th century. In other words, true "originality" today takes us back to our origins. If we understand how the gospel spread in the world of the first century, we will be better prepared to spread the gospel in this new world out "here." To seize tomorrow we must hold on to the past for dear life. We must cherish every scrap of history. Without cherishing and consulting our past, we constrain our future.

Much of the renewal literature is based on seizing the present and restoring churches to the *status quo ante*, to their condition prior to their problems ("when we had a full sanctuary") and decline. Yet God's desire for the church is that it enter a condition which is *more whole* and inhabit a place *more exciting* than anything it ever had in the past.

In Jesus' first public appearance, he leaned back to the prophet Isaiah to kick forward to the kingdom. The Messiah was sent "to bring good news to the poor . . . to proclaim release to the captives and recovery of sight to the blind, to let the oppressed go free, to proclaim the year of the Lord's favor."[52]

> *The further backward you look,*
> *the further forward you can see.*
>
> Winston Churchill[53]

Double-Boot No. 2

Closed system: Jesus is *the* Way, *the* Truth, and *the* Life.

Open system: No one can hamstring the Holy Spirit, which blows where it wills and brings Christ to life in the most surprising places and people.

Closed System: The Christian religion is more than a set of doctrines or a code of life. The Christian religion is Christ himself and life-in-Christ. Christ is the heart of God's revelation and salvation. Jesus is not merely a good way, a better way, or one way. Jesus is *the* Way, *the* Truth, and *the* Life. There is no salvation outside of Jesus the Christ.

Personally, it is beyond my comprehension why anyone would refuse God's free gift of love and grace. To decline the adventure of living Christ's life with him—well, to somebody like me who's crazy in love with Jesus, you'd have to be a complete moron.

In the 18th century, religious enthusiasts like the Methodists who believed like this were portrayed as insane. Some, like Alexander Cruden, the compiler of biblical concordances, were actually put away in madhouses.[54] The new (and true) context for the church is not a dominating and affluent presence, as we have experienced it in modern Western culture, but a persecuted and impoverished minority whose ways of living, loving, and thinking can expect to be mistaken for madness.

Here is the new, 21st-century context for those who would claim the name of Jesus—kidnapped, arrested, harassed, ridiculed ... even the Roman imperial turned-down thumb, "kill." A Chinese court has charged Hong Kong trader Li Guangquiang with using "an evil cult to damage a law-based society." His sentence is two years in prison. His crime? Bringing Bibles into mainland China.[55] The complicity between the US military and the Peruvian Air Force in shooting down a US missionary seaplane near the Colombian border (20 April 2001)—which killed 35-year-old Baptist missionary Veronica Bowers and her seven-month-old daughter, Charity—is a foretaste of our future.[56]

Too many Christians are living as if Nine-Eleven never happened.

What part of Nine-Eleven is so hard to understand? What part of Nine-Eleven don't you get, Christians?

There are people in your neighborhood who want to kill you.

There are people who hate me and despise all that I have come to cherish: freedom of religion, freedom of speech, freedom of press, freedom of Christ—those freedoms that define my very identity as a disciple and a citizen.

This hatred of Christianity did not await discovery in the caves of Afghanistan, where al Qaeda poems celebrating Nine-Eleven have been found by the US military, poems like this one signed by Mukhtar Said. The poem begins, "The cross has been smashed with the Koran's pick axe,/The hosts of the truth are striking with lances at the land of deviation, the abode of the devil."[57] Violent hatred of Christians has been well-telegraphed over the past decade in Islamic attempts to kill the Pope in 1995 when he visited the Philippines, to kill tourists in the Holy Land with a surprise bomb party scheduled for Christians visiting Jesus' baptismal site, and the episodic killings of Christians in Pakistan, Yemen, Sudan, Indonesia, and other parts of the Islamic world.

Nor do disciples of Jesus need only look for evidence of virulent anti-Christian sentiments in other religions or other lands. Look in your favorite book review section. When they aren't being attacked outright, novelists and poets with traces of Christianity in their writings are chided or scolded for "errors in logic." Yet Kim Stanley Robinson, the most significant science-fiction writer of the 20th century, doesn't get criticized for promoting Buddhism in his novels.[58]

Or look in your favorite university. Intellectuals today aren't doubting Christianity; they're despising it. One scholar summarizes being at a Christian eucharist as listening to "an account of a long-past torture session" of a god and then "pretending to eat the flesh of that god."[59] Another scholar admits that "in educated circles, religion is generally regarded as something malodorous. It has been more or less expunged from the high culture of the West."[60] In the same way that sexuality was once taboo in cultured circles, writes the novelist Nicholas Mosley, so now "to talk about life as if it had any meaning" is the new unmentionable.[61]

Or look in your backyard. A mother in Chapel Hill, North Carolina, told me of her

> *To be a Christian in polite society is to be a foreigner, an outsider. . . . It's as if you had told them about your colostomy bag.*
> Novelist Benjamin Cheever[62]

kids' coming home and singing a song they had learned in Sunday school, "Shine, Jesus, Shine." They taught it to the next-door neighbor's kids, who returned the favor the next day by teaching her kids' a new version of "Shine, Jesus, Shine" taught them by their parents: "Die, Jesus, Die." In the words of my friend Landrum Leavell III, "The Bible Belt broke."

The church-hop that is danced by one-in-six USAmericans can mask the mass exodus from Christianity that is well under way in the West. The ranks of USAmericans who call themselves Christian fell from 86% in 1990 to 77% in 2001.[63] Places once thriving with Christian communions (Europe, North America) are now floundering, while places once vacant of Christian influence (Africa, Asia, Latin America) are now kicking up a storm. This current recession in the West is perhaps the greatest recession in the church's history. What is being called Christianity's "shift in the center of gravity" means that Christianity is no longer centered in the West, nor is it any longer the religion of the West. According to Philip Jenkins, the "average" Christian in the world today "is not White fat cat in the United States or Western Europe, but rather a poor person, often unimaginably poor by Western standards,"[64] probably a poor, brown-skinned woman living in a third-world mega-city.

The head of the Roman Catholic Church in England and Wales has announced that as a background for people's lives, Christianity "has almost been vanquished."[65] Each day thousands of visitors visit the mother church of Anglicanism, Canterbury Cathedral. Each Sunday morning prayer service is attended by few more than a dozen worshipers. On any Sunday in London more people visit the local IKEA store than attend all the churches in the city combined. In France and Britain less than 10% of the population attend church at least once a month. Attendance in Scandinavian countries is less than 3%. In Amsterdam the Dutch Reformed Church is converting churches into luxury apartments just to pay the bills.

At a restaurant in Plymouth, Michigan, I eagerly picked up a booklet next to the menu entitled "Spiritual Guidance" and found hundreds of martini recipes. At a recent Covent Garden performance of Richard Wagner's opera *Parsifal*, Christian images were expunged, and the programme book celebrated those in the past who "chastized" Wagner's score by deleting or muting its "unequivocal Christian" stance.[66] After Nine-Eleven, museums "fulfilled their ultimate destiny and transformed themselves into religious sanctuaries." A brochure from one New York museum encouraged attendance at its shrine: "Your museum is a place of comfort, refuge, and spiritual salvation." The Austin Museum of Art summed up the situation: "During these trying and difficult times, art museums around the country are serving as places of congregation, sources of inspiration, and refuges of reflection for millions of Americans."[67] Museum historian Joseph Rykwert foresaw this:

> The sanctification of museums seems almost exactly contemporary to the secularizing of churches, so that the crowds of worshipers who have abandoned the churches now flow to museums. There they may admire the great masterpieces which the clergies of older religions commissioned from their contemporary artists and have since discarded or sold.[68]

The contrast between the collapse of Christianity in the West and the emergence of Christianity in the East could not be greater. In Scotland the percentage of Christians regularly attending church is less than 10%. In the Philippines that number is nearly 70%.[69] South Korea has almost four times as many Presbyterians as USAmerica. Although in Laos communist hard-liners have long enforced atheism to the point of forcing Christians to renounce their faith at the barrel of a gun, a Christian movement is growing by leaps and bounds.

Where the Spirit is most at work in the world is where Christianity is wanting to run wild, even in the choke of persecution and opposition. The greatest feature of Christianity in the southern world is the NUTS belief in miracles and a personal God who cares enough to "intervene directly in everyday life."[70] Christianity is in decline where faith is being passed on by churches for whom the Real Presence has vanished from the world, churches that no longer have confidence in the Scriptures or the Spirit, churches whose cold Christ can no longer warm the heart.[71] Christianity is growing where churches are crazy enough to expect that "everyday life," and every day, will be invaded by the unknown.[72]

> *How strange are my poems? Never strange enough,*
> *I'm sure, though what to me is homespun stuff*
> *May seem to others puzzling, even mad.*
>
> Poet Roy Fuller[73]

Open System: The Holy Spirit is what makes Christianity an open system. The Spirit bursts boundaries, breaks rules, surprises, and liberates. Wherever the Holy Spirit is, there is liberty.

It is the one and same Spirit who inspires us to an exclusive choice for the Lord Jesus Christ who also invites us to the unconditional acceptance of all peoples and to his presence in the most surprising places. God has revealed God's being through human history "at many times and in various ways."[74] Does Jesus shine only through Christians? Can't Jesus shine where he wants to shine? "There are many outside who appear to be inside, and many inside who appear to be outside," both Origen and Augustine observed in almost the same words.[75] An old Latin expression for this was *Novit Deus qui sunt ejus:* Only God knows who are his.

Perhaps it would be better if we spent more time learning from people of other faiths than denouncing them.[76] Aquinas taught that every truth, by whomsoever it is said, is from the Holy Spirit. John Calvin felt the same way. He argued that "if we reflect that the Spirit of God is the only fountain of truth, we will be careful, as we would avoid offering insult to him, not to reject or condemn truth wherever it appears. In despising the gifts, we insult the Giver."[77]

God is the source of all Truth, but also Beauty and Goodness. Whatever beauty, truth and goodness there is in the world, it is the result of receiving grace from the Source of all Truth, Beauty and Goodness.

> *God in His wisdom did not give all His gifts to Christians.*
> Nigel Goodwin[78]

For example, *Namaste*, a Hindu greeting means, "I honor the place in you where the entire universe resides." In this greeting (and farewell) hands are placed together in front of the heart, as a prayer, but also like a knife. Can you think of a better symbol of cutting through all the differences that keep us apart and occupying that shared place between all people across all cultures throughout the world? Can we not find with Islam and Hinduism some common ground on which we all can stand and walk together toward peace and justice?

For example, in native American languages there is no word for "religion." The word that comes closest is "the way you live."[79]

In a post-Christian culture, Christians have to learn how to coexist with those who hate us and are intolerant toward us. We must have tolerance toward the intolerant. After all, what does it mean to be tolerant? Does it mean that everybody is right? Everybody, that is, except the intolerant? In spite of its white heat of political correctness, this culture is deeply ambivalent about "tolerance," on the one hand making tolerance a core value and on the other hand boasting "zero tolerance" for certain behaviors and activities.

Death to the Intolerant
Bumper sticker

The best response to the actions of a closed system is to become as open as possible. When an open system starts to close in response to attacks from a closed system, the battle is already being lost. The answer to terror is courage. The answer to hatred is love. The answer to a closed system is to make it open in bigger, better, more radical ways than ever imagined. When a closed system makes the unthinkable thinkable, an open system must make the thinkable unthinkable. It must *not* do the predictable and thinkable: close up and shut down and keep out.

Double-Boot No. 3

Open system: inculturation.
Closed system: tribal identity.

Open System: The American Revolution was won by the Colonists partly because the British were categorical imperialists. The British knew the rules of war and refused to compromise those rules even when attacked by soldiers who could not have cared less about their combat categories and canons.

1. It was unethical to attack at night.
2. It was unethical to attack from many fronts at once.
3. It was unethical to hide and fight rather than wear red and stand up like a man.

When the world changes, new cultural categories emerge. Will the church insist on clinging to the old categories regardless, as the British did to their regret? Or will the church inculturate—that is, appropriate new categories to communicate the gospel more effectively? The Roman Catholic bishops from Indonesia composed this definition of "inculturation":

> Inculturation is the process of integrating Christian life experience within the local culture, so that this experience not only is experienced through local cultural elements, but also becomes an animating force giving that culture a new orientation and recreating it. Thus within that culture a new "communion" emerges, which in its turn enriches the Church universal.[80]

Inculturation must take place historically as well as geographically and ethnically. Just as non-Western Christianity must be defined first in non-Western terms,[81] as the Indonesian bishops argue, so non-modern Christianity must be defined first in non-modern terms.

Most congregations demand new converts undergo a "cultural circumcision"[82] that removes them from their native culture and returns them to a culture (modern) that is alien and strange. Christians are required to submit, not to a sex-change operation, but to a culture-change operation.[83]

> *[Change] has left the experience of elders useless to the tribulations of the young. Children, knowing how different their own lives will be, no longer look to parents as models and authorities; rather, parents now learn from their children.*
>
> Historian Arthur M. Schlesinger Jr.[84]

Incarnational Christianity is an absorbent culture, which enables other peoples to belong to it without damaging their own tribal or nationalistic identity. Here is a portrait of Christians of the second century, as described in the *Letter to Diognetus*. What strikes the author the most about

Christianity is its cultural adaptability: "Christians cannot be distinguished from the rest of the human race by country or language or customs. They do not live in cities of their own; they do not use a peculiar form of speech; they do not follow an eccentric manner of life."[85]

Unfortunately, multinational corporations are proving to be more "incarnational" than churches. To be sure, we need better versions of globalization than the one that is now in place. Various scholars have detailed how multinationals often operate around the world with little accountability and hold undeveloped countries in the grip of tyranny.[86] There needs to be change in corporate conduct and sense of responsibility, both to the environment and to the peoples of the world.

Globalization: For some the mere word *globalization* is enough to cause riots; for others it is the path to righteousness and peace. The truth is neither. But in spite of what "globaphobes" would tell us, globalization need not equate colonialism. Globalization can actually work to eradicate poverty. Want to keep the poor poor? Keep them out of the global economy. A NUTS perspective on globalization means fewer goods than freedoms, but globalization has the best hope of turning abundance to an advantage for the poor.

In fact, far from stomping on and stamping out local cultures, globalization works to preserve niche communities and cultures. Think of eBay and what people collect. How do beekeepers or Welsh-speakers connect? Multinationals either adapt to local tastes or die; skilled inculturation in shifting cultural and political climates is now a global requirement. The KFC brand indigenizes itself in Japan with tempura crispy strips. KFC indigenizes itself in Thailand with fresh rice with soy or sweet chili sauce. KFC indigenizes itself in Holland with potato-and-onion croquettes. KFC indigenizes itself in France with pastries. KFC indigenizes itself in northern England with gravy and potatoes. KFC indigenizes itself in China with chicken that gets spicier the farther inland you travel.[87] In spite of the fact that a KFC value meal is the equivalent of about six hours of the average person's salary, KFC opened its 500th restaurant in mainland China in early October 2001. By the time you read this, there will be over 600 KFCs and 65 Pizza Huts in at least 130 cities across China.[88] (By the way, does anyone remember anymore that KFC once stood for Kentucky Fried Chicken?)

Every leader, every church can inculturate in varying degrees. Not too long ago I worshiped where I thought I would find traditional worship at its highest and finest. It had been a rough week, with all sorts intellectual and spiritual skirmishes with disciples who oppose screen culture and attack people like me for "dumbing down the gospel." One pastor told me that if he insisted on a screen in his church's sanctuary and moved to more EPIC models of ministry, he would lose his church. My brain felt that it needed a sauna, so I decided to immerse my soul in worship where tradition is most cherished and preserved: St. Patrick's Cathedral in New York City.

Guess what I discovered during High Mass at St. Patrick's Cathedral, the very residence of the pope when he is in the United States? Screens, screens, and more screens. In fact, I counted 10 screens—and those were just the ones I could see from where I was sitting. At least twice that number lay scattered throughout the sanctuary and nestled in the statuary.

Closed System: Who can forget the pronouncement of Parson Thwackum in Henry Fielding's novel *Tom Jones?* "When I mention religion, I mean the Christian religion, and not only the Christian religion, but the Protestant religion, and not only the Protestant religion, but the Church of England."[89] If Henry Fielding were writing *Tom Jones* today, he might further niche "religion" into the "gay/lesbian evangelical wing of the Church of England."

Trade agreements that integrate national economies, cross-border investments—these open systems have unifying economies. But those things that make a people special—culture, politics, religion—are getting more unique and going in opposite directions.

In an open system, identity and attention are the primary drivers. That's why the more global we become, the more tribal we act. The more globalism turns us into swans or little "me's," the more we gather together like seals or little "we's." Swans keep their distance from one another; seals do just the opposite, hanging all over each other with little social or personal space.

The future will be filled with ethnic, national, religious, and racial pride. We gather in tribes: Go to a football game, and there's the Tampa Bay Buccaneers tribe, the Green Bay Packers tribe, and so on; go to a NASCAR race, and there's the Earnhardt tribe, the Petty tribe, and . . . . Can you name any ethnic group anywhere that is not trying to preserve and enhance cultural identity? In fact, the renaissance of interests in cultural identities is one of the distinguishing features of our day. The Italians are becoming more Italian, the Germans more German, the Mexicans more Mexican. We are hunkering down within our trusted circles, investing time in tribal relationships as never before.

USAmerica is the first truly global nation. Multicultural is our ethnicity. In my lifetime it's not even a toss-up: USAmerica has been changed more profoundly by globalization than USAmerica has changed the globe. In other words, globalization does not mean Americanization. The so-called "Americanization of the planet" has to do with the only most superficial decisions—what sneakers or jeans do you wear under the robe, or what nectar do we drink, or what . . . ? Even then, everything is becoming more global.

I may start every day with orange juice and coffee, but my favorite juice is mango, and my favorite caffeinated drink is Moroccan tea.

We are not fashioning the world in our own image. The world is refashioning the US in its own image. The dominant Anglo culture is not remaining normative. There are now 329 languages spoken in the USA. In the archdiocese of New York, Mass is said in 35 different languages. There are 375 Islamic schools in the US. One scholar talks about the "Asianization" of America.[90] Still not convinced? Need more examples? Look at how immigration is changing Miami Dade County. Listen to all the diverse voices. Or listen to how Harvard's Diana Eck begins her book *A New Religious America*:

> The huge white dome of a mosque, with its minarets, rises from the cornfields just outside Toledo, Ohio. . . . A great Hindu temple with elephants carved in relief at the doorway stands on a hillside in the western suburbs of Nashville. A Cambodian Buddhist temple and monastery with a hint of a Southeast Asian roofline is set in the farmlands southeast of Minneapolis.[91]

Not only are we not monolithic, but our race to diversity is breath-taking.[92] My eight-year-old daughter's name is Soren, to honor her Norwegian mother. Her best buddies at her Montessori school? Their names are Omri, Jhuanna, Ursula, Amelia. The Montessori school on Orcas Island is not a melting/smelting pot but a *mosaic* with individual tiles. Up close, individual colors dominate. But step back, see the big picture, and the borders blend into one another. You tell me: Does the mortar separate, or join, the tiles? The metaphor is even more dynamic than this, for it is now a moving *mosaic*—a motion picture with moving tiles constantly shifting, a dynamic and ever-changing kaleidoscope of cultures.[93]

The difference between the old tribalism and the new tribalism is that in the new tribalism, those in the Church of England or "the Christian Church" (of whatever "wing") don't ostracize or demonize those of other tribes. What is the matter with differences between Christians? How do differences among Christians matter?

"Harmonious difference" is the essence of unity—an understanding of unity that the church of all places has a hard time understanding. As much as the church likes to recite, "Blessed are you when men shall persecute you," we find it very difficult to realize that to the eyes and ears of a good many people, it is the church that persecutes rather than is persecuted.

The "persecuted" can be either within or without. The first accusation against Christianity's first martyr, Stephen, was that he had bad-mouthed the church. He said that true religion was not temple-based or law-bound.

> **Leave Christians alone, they'll kill each other.**
>
> George Bernard Shaw[94]

The second accusation against Stephen was that he would "change the customs Moses handed down to us."[95] In other words, he was going to change the status quo and mess with "tradition." Leaders who move the church from its temple-based, law-bound, status-quo condition will be persecuted.

But persecution can also be directed at those without. Caribbean novelist Caryl Phillips is known for his "Phillips' Manifesto":

> The old static order in which one people speaks down to another, lesser, people is dead. The colonial, or postcolonial, model has collapsed. In its place we have a new

world order in which there will soon be one global conversation with limited participation open to all, and full participation available to none.[96]

We are now all global citizens. We must become global Christians. How many people in our churches are studying other cultures and learning other languages? How many are taking mission trips abroad? How many US Christians hold a passport? How many can locate South Africa on a map? How about the Persian Gulf? Try the Pacific Ocean?

The need for the church to embody Christ's love for this new global world, however, does not mean that tribes becomes less important. Just the opposite. It does mean, however, that all tribes must become better at loving than hating.

My tribal identities are first and foremost spiritual—Christianity—and secondarily social and political—USAmerica. I am unabashedly proud of the fact that non-Western peoples are adopting from my political tribe such "Western" ideas as universal education, the equality of women, human rights, due process of law, private property, self-determination, and religious freedom.

Not all cultural imperialism is bad. The Taliban—perhaps the most misogynistic regime in history—were wrong about women. Jesus is right. Communism, which cost the lives of between 85 and 100 million people in the 20th century—more than the losses in both World Wars[97]—was wrong about not protecting the individual. Jesus is right. There are Christian subcultures of violence and hatred that are as virulent as terrorist organizations like Egypt's Islamic Jihad, Algeria's GIA, Yemen's Aden Abyan Islamic Army, Afghanistan's al Qaeda. They are wrong. Jesus is right. The systematic stereotyping and degrading of Easterners has been called "Orientalism." The systematic stereotyping and dehumanizing of Westerners has been called "Occidentalism."[98] Both are wrong. In Mererani, Tanzania, Imam

Sheik Omari lectures students at the new mosque Taqwa that "Islam teaches us that your body is a weapon."[99] Christianity teaches that your body is a temple. Imam Sheik Omari is wrong. Jesus is right.

There are universal standards and truths that hold across cultures. There are philosophical differences between "how things are for me" and "how it is." In fact, putting yourself in someone else's place is a strategy of absolute truth, not relativism. One of the biggest challenges the church faces today is rescuing people who have become orphans of truth, lost in the disorienting maze of relativism.

Relativism has been relativized by absolute truth: Jesus Christ. But beliefs in absolute truths are not necessarily strategies of truth. Some of the greatest evildoers in history were moral absolutists, not relativists: Hitler, Jim Jones, Pol Pot, Osama bin Laden, Timothy McVeigh, to name a few.

In Doris Lessing's novel *The Sweetest Dream,* the character Sylvia says, "And when there's a massacre or a tribal war or a few missing millions, all they have to do is to murmur, 'It's a different culture.'"[100] The relativists' cry, "All meaning is relative!" self-destructs—or better, implodes—for it means that relativism is a meaningless discourse that itself is relative and can be deconstructed. The notion that we "ought" not to say "ought" is a double bind. Nothing is any more "faith-free" than "fat-free." Even relativism is a faith stance, albeit an autistic one.[101]

There *is* such a thing as truth as against your truth or my truth. Religious freedom is true, and religious oppression is false. Democracy is a better form of government than totalitarianism. Difference is salubrious, and sameness is unhealthy.

But truth always sparkles like a diamond. It needs to be looked at from a variety of angles, from multiple facets, for its wholeness to be understood. All angels have angles. In the African-American tradition there is a saying that there are four sides to every story: his side, her side, the inside, and the outside.

Truth is technicolor. Truth is traduced when reduced to monochrome.

> Here in the Brave New World's embrace
> I watch the parade begin
> Searching for one familiar face
> And I wonder where I fit in
> How will I know if there's a place
> For me in the Brave New World?
>
> Styx, "Brave New World"[102]

Concluding Coda

> *"Peace be with you!*
> *As the Father has sent me,*
> *I am sending you . . .*
> *[into this emerging culture]."*
>
> Jesus[103]

Whatever your character, whatever your context, "Be There."

Or, in a more current version of these two words, "I'm In!"[104]

One of the greatest psychological transitions for post-modern natives is to go from the shrug of "whatever" to the nod of "I'm in!"

In the words of the Mitsubishi commercial, "Are You In?"

The original, Ur-version of Be-There/I'm-In incarnational theology? I AM.

The greatest definition of an incarnational leader is found in the Great Commandment. A leader is one who loves the Image-made-Flesh who is "I Am" with all his/her mind, body, spirit, and who loves _____ (you fill in the blank—Oregonians? Appalachians? East Hamptons? South Dakotans? Pre-Christians? postmoderns?) as himself/herself.

Be There or Be Square

Happy Days' (ABC)
Richie Cunningham

Arguably the most difficult phrase to translate in the Bible is the answer God gave to Moses when he asked God, "What is your name?"

The most common translation is, "I am who I am." Toward the end of his life, one of the greatest Hebrew scholars of the 20th century, Martin Buber, admitted that the phrase "I AM who I AM" was probably a mistranslation. After a lifetime of study, Buber came to a different translation. God's name is best translated, Buber argued, as "I will be present as I will be present." Or else, "I Shall Be There."[105]

God's name is less "I AM who I AM" than "I Shall Be There."[106]

> *Where can I go from your Spirit?*
> *Or where can I flee from your presence?*
> *If I ascend to heaven, you are there;*
> *If I make my bed in Sheol, you are there.*
> *If I take the wings of the morning*
> *and settle at the farthest limits of the sea,*
> *even there your hand shall lead me,*
> *and your right hand shall hold me fast.*
> The Inescapable God: A Psalm[107]

I Shall Be There: Being God means to "Be There" in your pain. Being God means to "Be There" in your doubt. Being God means to "Be There" in your blowouts.

We have a God who has promised to "Be There" for us.

Being God means to "Be There in our future." In this emerging future, God will "Be There."

Will we "be there" too?

The poor migrant farm worker named Tom Joad from John Steinbeck's novel *The Grapes of Wrath* is a classic character in Western fiction. "The Ballad of Tom Joad" was first written and sung by folksinger Woody Guthrie in 1940. Bruce Springsteen gave the ballad a more electronic sound in 1995. Rage Against the Machine recently reinvented the song with heavy-metal shadings. No matter who interprets the song, however, the power of the lyrics shines through.

> Now Tom said; "Ma, whenever ya see a cop beatin' a guy
> Wherever a hungry newborn baby cries
> Wherever there's a fight against the blood and hatred in the air
> Look for me, ma, I'll be there . . .
> Wherever somebody is strugglin' to be free
> Look in their eyes, ma, You'll see me."[108]

Or, in the words of another song I grew up singing, "When the Roll Is Called Up Yonder," will you . . . Be There?

Can you Be There then, if you can't Be There now?

part 2

Relational Discipleship
WITH ALL

Too many Christians are no longer fishers of men but keepers of the aquarium.
—Radio commentator Paul Harvey

It had been a long morning. My consultation with the leadership team of one of the most dynamic and innovative churches in the Pacific Northwest had been invigorating, but exhausting.

The amenities of the lodge where we were staying didn't help. They were those of the 1950s: the coffee instant, the bread sliced, the eggs powdered.

During the lunch hour I ducked out and hit the rainy pavement of the quaint streets of the seaside community of Cannon Beach, Oregon. I saw the sign I was looking for: "Cabana Café." Someone had already tipped me off that they served "great coffee," and as I walked the little path to the door, I sniffed in my mind the robust aroma of ground coffee.

The door was locked. I pulled harder. Still locked. Then I saw a hand-written sign inserted into the screen door: "Out to Lunch. Be back at 1:30." Still not believing my eyes, I walked to the front window and peeked in. Sure enough, the lights were on, but no one was inside. Then my eye caught another handmade notice: "Store for sale. Great business location and opportunity."

A café closed for lunch. A proprietor who was more con-cerned about feeding himself and taking care of his own stomach than serving hungry people walking the streets looking for a place to eat. A restaurant that didn't know what business it was in.

No wonder he was going out of business.

No wonder 75% of the churches in USAmerica are going out of business—either declining or dying. "Out to Lunch" says it all. We're so busy feeding our faces, taking care of our own needs, that we're ignoring the hungry and thirsty who are being sent away empty.

I am often asked how a church can better communicate its message to a "lost world." Yet ministry doesn't begin with being understood, but with under-standing others. Have we really done our homework to understand the spiritual quests of people who are out there on the streets of this 21st-century world?

> *No persecutor or foe in two thousand years has wreaked such havoc on the church as has modernity.*
>
> John Drane[1]

You tell me: Is your church talking *at* or talking *to* your culture? Is your church Open? Or is it Out to Lunch?

For the church to be "open" to this emerging culture requires a move from a *reformational* to a *missional* para-digm.[2] A reformational paradigm is fixed on the message: getting right what we think about God. A reformational par-adigm focuses on the church and differences between Christians—the marks of a pure and true church versus a false church. A reformational paradigm assumes Christen-dom thinking.[3] Christianity has been in the reformational paradigm for 500 years.

The *missional* paradigm is fixed on methods: communi-cating what God has done in and for us; communicating the divine presence through worship, the arts, and commu-nity. The missional church focuses on the world where people don't believe the gospel in the least.

Purity is the goal if you're in the reformational paradigm.

Communication is the goal if you're in the missional paradigm.

The biblical model is both reformational *and* missional. But the reformation occurs in the context of being in mis-sion: how do we mediate the saving grace of Jesus to a fallen world? Once again, the corporate world seems to be more aware of what's involved than does the church. In the words of philosopher/business consultant Peter Koestenbaum, "More than ever, we should celebrate the artists in business, the reformers in life, and the missionaries in organizations."[4]

Christianity must give up its Christendom mind-set and become a missionary movement once again. Church leaders must give up their "pastoral" headsets and become cross-cultural missionaries once again.

If you're in mission, God will give you the wherewith-alls. *With* is the relationship word. *All* is the missional word. There have been, and continue to be, "holy wars" of misunderstanding about these two simple words *with* and *all*.

In words of the Jewish Shema, spoken daily by the observant—words I like to call "God for Dummies"—God is to be loved "with all" . . .

> with all your heart,
> with all your soul,
> with all your strength,
> and with all your mind.[5]

Only 1% of USAmerican churches are growing because of reaching normal people for Jesus. The vast majority aren't growing at all (75% are in decline or have leveled off), and those that are growing (24%) are basically recycling the saints through church hopping and shopping ("migrant worshipers").

To "Be There With All" is to be a OnePercenter.

To "Be There With All" is to join the most exclusive club in the world: The OnePercent Club.

Wherever you are, be all there. Live to the hilt every situation you believe to be the will of God.
Missionary Aviation Fellowship pilot Jim Elliot[6]

"It's a Nuthouse": WITH

One night in a dream I saw the Lord, who said to me,
"What do you desire, Bayezid?"
"That which you desire, my God!"
"O Bayezid, it is you I desire, as you desire me."
—Ninth-century Indian mystic Bayezid Bistami[7]

Novelist/playwright Christopher Isherwood opened the door to let in his dinner guest, playwright George Axelrod. Isherwood apologized for his coughing, admitting that he had a bad cold and probably should have canceled dinner. Instantly George retorted, "My dear Christopher, . . . any cold of yours is a cold of mine."[8]

In this incident between two great literary minds of the 20th century, we have a manifestation of our third little word with planetary consequences: *with*.

Have you ever noticed how important this one little word *with* was to Jesus? Jesus was constantly asking people to "be with" him. Jesus went up on the mountain, prayed all night, and chose some disciples to "be with" him. He promised that where "two or more" would gather together, there he would "be with" them. In fact, we read in the gospels that Jesus "appointed twelve—designating them apostles—that they might *be with* him and that he might send them out to preach."[9]

Sometimes Jesus focused that "withness" inwardly: "The kingdom of God is within you."[10] Sometimes he pointed the "withness" outward: Jesus relished sharing the experiences of life "with" others.

It is for this reason that John Shea once called Jesus "the Spirit Master" rather than "Teacher" or "Rabbi." For Shea, Jesus as teacher

> suggests distance and impartiality. The teacher is someone who disseminates information; in this case, a body of beliefs are passed along. He or she has mastered some subject matter and is about the business of organizing it and passing it along. The student is a secondary object of attention. As teachers often say with a shrug, students either "get the material or they don't."[11]

In contrast, Shea writes, in Jesus' teaching the communication of spirit is paramount.

> He does not teach lessons; he primarily encounters people. He is passionately person-centered. When he tells his disciples to come away with him to an out-of-the-way place, he is not only suggesting rest and relaxation (Mk. 6:30). He wants time with them. Just "being with" his disciples is an essential ingredient of his way of teaching and their way of learning. Jesus engages the total person. . . . Certainly Jesus instructs his disciples on the level of perceptions, attitudes and actions. But in and through this communication a deeper reality is handed on. The very spirit of Jesus is communicated. This happens through symbiosis and osmosis. They walk and talk and eat and work with Jesus; and there is a slow assimilation of how he sees and hears the world. This process is partly conscious and partly unconscious.
>
> . . . Once the spirit is shared, the person of the Master lives on in the person of the disciple. . . . The master is not satisfied with mental connections. The disciple must experience the teaching physically and spiritually.

... This gives us a clue to the depth of the relationship between Jesus the master and anyone who would be his disciple. Jesus wants the disciple to experience the reality he knows; he does not want to pass along the conclusions of his experience. In the deepest moment it is not a sharing of belief and theology but an introduction to Abba. If Abba is met, shared beliefs follow, flowers out of the same soil. All knowledge must be realized. Realized knowledge changes perception and overflows into action.[12]

Presbyterian pastor E. Stanley Ott is so struck by all Jesus' "with's" that he raises Jesus' "withness" to a cardinal principle of ministry: "ministry team life, itself, is a complex expression of the with-me principle."[13] Granted, it is hard for individualistic moderns to understand how very primary "withness" was for Jesus. But the incarnation is withness stuff. The crucifixion is withness stuff. The resurrection is withness stuff. In fact, withness is the primary spiritual orientation of ministry.

Christian psychologist Paul Welter is another one so impressed by all this "withness" that he proposes a "new" approach to helping that is not based on helper-helpee, but on Jesus' person-being-with-person technique of "helping."[14] Welter's aim is to equip ordinary, everyday people to help others rather than leaving it up to "professionals" in the "helping professions."

The key theological term of the 21st century is relationship. *With* is the relationship word, and *withness* advances a relational framework, a relational poetics, a relational missiology. Nothing that exists does so without participation in the being of God. There can be no truth, beauty, or goodness without participation in a relationship with the divine. But relationship with the transcendent assumes participation in the temporal. To be a person is to experience the "withness" of God and others.

The challenge of the church in the 21st century is to make itself less of an institution and more of a community;

less a place that asks, "What can you do for us?" and more a place that asks, "What can we do for you?"; less a place focused on better facilities and more a place focused on faith upgrades; less led by people prone to call a meeting than by people prone to start a conversation.

Basically the church has only two things to offer the world: Christ and community. Yet we have heard the word *community* so often that the word itself can become a blockage to its true meaning. That's why I prefer words such as *connectedness* and *relationships* to *community*.

Only in relationship do we discover God. Only in relationship do we discover what it means to be human. Only in relationship do we discover anything. Chase Bank is right, even if it did steal our line: "The right relationship is everything." But the "right relationship" is not with a bank.

> *"Who is he who will devote himself to be close to me?" declares the LORD?*
> Jeremiah[15]

We know from the new physics that nothing exists independent of relationships. We should have known this first from Scripture, where we learn that relationship is the ultimate reality of the universe. The covenant theme in Jewish history, in which relationship precedes identity, is continued in the Second Testament and culminates in Jesus the Christ.

It's all about relationships.

God's Own "Withness" Is Revealed As Trinity

The doctrine of the Trinity puts relationships at the very heart of the divine. If Christian theology is an ontology of love, then it is also an ontology of relationships. Theologian Paul Fiddes has done the most to outline a participatory doctrine of God in his superb study of the Trinity. Because the Trinity is less a model for human beings' activities and more a way of engagement with divine being and activity, Fiddes advocates a view of "persons *as* relationships in God" rather than "persons in relationship" with God.[16]

The distinction is subtle, but profound. God created us out of this need for "withness." Just as God knew it was not good for God to be alone, so God knew it was not good for "the man" to be alone. God is *not* a "self-contained absolute,"[17] but a self-emptying communion.

Even God is not an isolate, but a participant. "God is not God because God holds the divine identity and does not let anyone else have it," states theologian Arthur C. McGill. "That is the mark of Satan. God is God because God *shares* that identity, The Father with the Son, and through the Son, the Father with us."[18]

The mystery of the universe is not found in isolates but in participants and wholes. Reality is composed of nested relationships—wholes within wholes (holons), each one having its own integrity yet without integrity unless part of the larger wholes within which each is embedded. In this holographic withness of creation, everything is revealed as relationship. There are not parts, only participants. Isolate anything from the web of relationships, and it ceases to exist. "Existence is co-existence" is how Jewish theologian Abraham Heschel put it. God less enters into relationship than God *is* relationship.[19]

How did the apostle John express God's withness? "God is love."[20]

After writing 33 novels and some 200 short stories and garnering the Nobel Prize for literature, this is how Arab novelist Naguib Mahfouz summarizes his faith in God: "I am love. Were it not for me the water would dry up, the air would become putrid, and death would strut about in every corner."[21]

Does love's witness emanate from you like the scent from a rose?

> Take away love, and our earth is a tomb.
> Poet Robert Browning[22]

Our Very "Be" Depends on This Word *With*

No person is set and sealed off in a physical body. Every one of us is affected and influenced by the thoughts and actions of others. Thanks to the new science, we now know that mind affects matter (psychokinesis),[23] that mind influences mind at great distances (non-localism),[24] that mind operates not only beyond space but beyond time,[25] that prayer has direct therapeutic consequences,[26] and that "peak experiences" when "the whole universe is perceived as an integrated and unified whole"[27] are worth taking seriously.

No one can stand on their own two feet because we need more than two feet on which to stand. There is an old African saying, "We are, therefore I am." The USArmy discovered the we-ness of me-ness and designed an advertising campaign around it. One of the most prize-winning campaigns in the history of advertising—"Be All You Can Be . . . Join the Army"—no longer captures the attention much less the imagination of potential recruits. The new appeal features the withness of "An Army of One."

The word *free,* when traced back to its origins in the ancient Indo-European language (the mother of modern Western languages), yields the root word *pri,* which means "to love." This same root gave rise to a host of relationship words, including *friend.* A "free" man was not set loose from entangling ties and relationships. Rather, a "free" man *chose* relationships out of love and loyalty and was known for allegiance and obedience to those "freely chosen" relationships and responsibilities.[28]

In our new identity as disciples of Jesus we live in a nutty state of wisdom that Arthur McGill calls *"receiving without having, a constant receiving."*[29] McGill's provocative meditation on Paul's one question—"What have you that you did not receive? If then you received it, why do you boast as if it were not a gift?"[31]—has been ignored and rejected by a modernity that lacked the discipline of receiving. If there is "one thing needed" by NUTS disciples, it is this discipline of receiving that which has been given.

If not for others, how could I be myself?

Epigraph to the Acknowledgments in Hillel Schwartz, *The Culture of the Copy*[30]

The discipline of receiving extends to our very "being." We receive ourselves from our relationships. We less "possess" an identity than "receive" an identity from our witness. If we cannot handle the posture of receiving, we cannot share the blessed state of relatedness.

The craziness of witness is this: We can't show ourselves our own face or tell ourselves our own story. We need others to show us our face and tell us our story. Most importantly, we need God to reveal to us our own face and tell us our personal story. That is why storytelling is such a communal and interactive event. We can't see our own face or understand our own story until other people interact with our face and story. Until our story is connected to God's story, until our being is in a state of openness to God's being and to the fullness of being, there can be no true Christian character.

What makes us all different is the pattern of our vibrations. You are never the same person you were five years ago. All the atoms that made up your body then are gone, replaced by new ones. You're a totally new you.

Or are you?

It's not the atoms that make you. It's the connections and patterns of those atoms. So you don't have the same head you did five years ago in terms of atoms, but in terms of connecting patterns you do.

What gives things character is resonance. Sympathetic vibrations are what makes a bass drum different from a bassoon. It's the same with people. What shapes character are those things, those "withnesses," with which you resonate: books and films, family and friends, and most important, Jesus the Christ.

Show me the withnesses of your life—your connections and patterns of relationships—and I'll show you who you are. We know the first half of the popular networking aphorism: "It's not what you know, but who you know." But there's another half: "It's not what you know, but who you know, who knows you, and what is it that they know about you."

The poet W. H. Auden contends that "one can't talk about good and bad people, but only about good and bad relationships."[32] Good discipleship and bad discipleship have a similar base. So also do good and bad ministry. The first call of a priest is not to ordained ministry, but to a relationship with God through Jesus the Christ. We are in ministry, not because of what our relationships can do for others, but because of what God's relationship has done and is doing in us.

Our Continued Being Depends on This Word *With*

The "other" is not another. The "other" is I. Selflessness is the only path to happiness. Or, in the words of Wei Wu Wei, "Why are you unhappy? Because 99.9% of everything you do is for yourself—and there isn't one."[33]

India and Indiana help determine how severe the tragic floods of Bangladesh will be. What's left of the orca whale population in Puget Sound is dying because of smokestacks in China. How polluted the Nile basin is depends on the actions of 10 countries. How polluted the Mediterranean is depends on the decisions of 20 countries. Some 261 of the world's rivers are shared by two or more countries. Everything you do affects me, and everything I do affects you.

This withness is even more true of Jesus' crazy follow-ers, for "in Christ we who are many form one body, and each member *belongs* to all the others."[34] Your hurt pierces me; my despair drapes all over you; your silence rouses me. This sense of mutuality is like the hidden side of the moon to moderns, but as thrilling to postmoderns as man's first landing on the moon.

Withness was the light of day to our ancestors. A mem-ber of the Dagara tribe, Sobonfu Somé, tells compelling sto-ries about Dano, the West African village where she grew up.

> In the village, . . . every morning when you wake up somebody will come and ask you, "Did you hear something sweet last night?" and if you remain silent or you say no, then the person will get worried because something is wrong. If you didn't hear something good, it means that something sour must have taken the place of the good. They will then get to the bottom of that problem before it gets out of control.[35]

There is a saying in Dagara that "trouble becomes scared when voiced."

> When you talk about problems, these problems start to hate you, and usually we are safe if a problem hates us. This is one reason why in the indigenous context, people don't mind verbalizing what is troubling them. They know that even if people don't know how to fix it right away, the simple fact that a problem has been wrapped in words can scare it away.[36]

Even something as private and exclusionary as marriage is seen in the village of Dana as a withness event. They see the entire community as entering into the wedding covenant, and marriage ceremonies provide rituals for oth-ers to renew their vows and marry each other once again. The wedding is less a way of soliciting gifts than enlisting support for the troubles of the future. In the West, everyone likes to attend weddings but when trouble comes to a marriage, the people who showed up at the wedding are nowhere to be found at the showdown. No one wants to get involved. In the Dagara tribe, "when trouble hits, they [those who showed up at the wedding] will be the first ones to show up."[37]

Heightening Hunger for Withness

People are getting "stickier." Normal people are hungry for what really matters, the "real" meaning of existence, the "real estate" of life: not property and possession, but relationships, family, and friends. This 21st-century stickiness not only will never dry, but will keep getting more gooey and gluey. "Withness" is the 21st-century tar baby from which attempts to escape only makes things worse.

The stickiness is everywhere. Bryan Dyson, the former CEO of Coca-Cola, gave a speech in which he asked his hearers to imagine life as a game in which you are juggling five balls in the air.

> You name them: work, family, health, friends, and spirit. You will soon understand that work is a rubber ball. If you drop it, it will bounce back. But the other four balls—family, health, friends, and spirit—are made of glass. If you drop one of these, they will be irrevocably scuffed, marked, nicked, damaged, or even shattered. They will never be the same.[38]

Forget the buzz that divorce is at epidemic proportions. The divorce rate has been slowly declining since its peak in 1981, when it reached a rate of 5.3 divorces per 1,000 people. In 2000 the divorce rate dropped to 4.1, the lowest since 1972 and lower even than in 1946 after World War II.[39]

When all is said and done, what do we end up with? What do we leave behind if we haven't lived a wasted life?

When "death taps us on the shoulder and asks us to encapsulate a life by its loves,"[40] what will survive of us? The real estate of life is "its loves"—love relationships with God, with family and friends, with creatures and creation.

The penny-saved-is-a-penny-earned philosophy of life was critiqued brilliantly by Karl Marx, who prophesied correctly that the government of men would be replaced by the administration of things. Where Marx went awry was his attack on private capital and investment income. He thought their existence was a blight on the planet. The blight is that not enough people on the planet have them.[41]

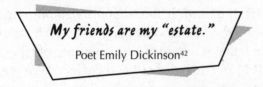

My friends are my "estate."

Poet Emily Dickinson[42]

Novelist Iris Murdoch once suggested that a good question to ask of any philosopher is, "What are you afraid of?" It's a good question to ask of anyone, as every therapist knows. After Nine-Eleven, the biggest fear of the largest number of people became living disconnected lives. People began celebrating values and things that help them connect: from comfort foods like pizza and popcorn to "comfort toys" like Lincoln Logs and TinkerToys, the surprise Christmas gifts of 2001.

One day, after a lifetime of cramming for the Final Exam at Judgment Day, you and I are not going to be asked, "What were your 'positions' about government, genetic engineering, or glossalalia?" When it comes to our Life Review, what will the questions be? How many books did you write? How many A's did you get? How many resolutions did you pass? Isn't the Life Review question "What is your heart?"

The exam is not about beliefs but about relationships. At the final judgment we learn that our relationship to God is measured in terms of our withness relationships with God and with others.

The term for "personhood" in the Zulu-Xhosa tongue in Africa is *ubuntu*. The concept of *ubuntu* lies behind one of the most remarkable social inventions in the history of humanity—South Africa's Truth and Reconciliation Commission (TCR). As defined by Nelson Mandela, "*Ubuntu* means humanity—to be human—compassionate—to be able to put yourself in the place of others, especially those vulnerable in society." The core belief of *ubuntu* is this: "*umntu ngumntu ngabantu, motho ke motho ba batho ba bangwe*," which translates as "a human being is a human being because of other human beings."[43] To out this in shorthand English: "We are, therefore I am." *Ubuntu* is now appreciated as a controlling component of the African worldview, "a guide for social conduct as well as a philosophy of life."[44]

Ubuntu is another way of talking about withness. What does it mean for a shepherd to be "with" a flock? It means more than proximity. Withness requires participation in each other's lives, bearing or carrying "one another's burdens."[45] The Indo-European background of *carry* or *bear* is *bher*, a word signifying the relationship of a mother and a birthing child. Withness requires transference, labor, pain, identification, and connection on all shared levels of life.[46]

To learn *ubuntu* is to learn a spiritual alphabet of withness that builds relationships. In a submarine, discordant relationships can kill you, and planet Earth is a submarine swimming in space. I have learned this from a decade of living on Orcas Island, Washington. Island living requires the cultivation of an alphabet of virtues—affirmation, blessing, compassion, discipline, empathy, forbearance, grace, humility, identification, and so on. On an island you can't pick fights or hold feuds. You learn to exercise and eat with people you don't like. No matter how unpleasant the people, you can't escape them. Any "enemies" would be the parents of your children's best friends. Serious divisions could destroy the town.

Serious divisions are destroying the world. Gideon Byamugisha is a priest in the Church of Uganda and the first priest in Africa to declare he was living with HIV. On a continent where every 15 seconds someone dies of an AIDS-related illness, Reverend Gideon argues that

> AIDS isn't just a disease. It is a symptom of something deeper which has gone wrong within the global family. It reveals our broken relationships, between individuals, communities and nations. It exposes how we treat and support each other, and where we are silent. It shows us flaws in the way we educate each other, and the way we look at each other as communities, races, nations, classes, sexes, and between age groups. AIDS insists that it is time for us to sit down and address all the things we have been quiet about—sexuality, poverty, and the way we handle our relationships from the family level to the global level.[47]

"Third World" is a terrible phrase. There is only One World. We like to talk about functioning in different worlds: the world of work, the world of home, the world of sports, the world of cyberspace, the world of finance. But if the holy lunacy of *ubuntu* is understood, there is really only one world. We can talk about having different lives: the life of a husband, a father, an employee, a volunteer. But holy lunacy says they are really all one world. We can talk about the world of Islam, the Christian world, the Jewish world, the world of Buddhism. But holy lunacy says the world is really only one. The world of Islam *is* the Christian world and vice versa. Nine-Eleven was the day the world learned just how connected and small it really is. A religious teacher living in a cave in Afghanistan can bring the world to its feet—and to its knees.

The craziest thing Jesus ever said was to love our enemies. We talk about relationships with "friends" and "enemies." For NUTS disciples, the two are one. If a good actor can be defined, as Sacha Guitry says, as "one who says 'I love you!' more convincingly to an actress he doesn't love than to the actress he does,"[48] then a good Christian can be defined as one who says, "I love you!" more devoutly to an enemy than to a friend. After all, the early church prayed for Nero.

> It's not enough to hate your enemy. You have to understand how the two of you bring each other to a deep completion.
>
> Novelist
> Don DeLillo[51]

In today's warfare, victims are unlikely ever to see the people who kill them. In previous wars, battles were hand-to-hand struggles. There are authentic reports of adversaries bayoneting each other simultaneously and being found later on the battlefield locked together in death.[49] That, to me, is a very striking theological image of NUTS wisdom. We live together and we die together—friends and enemies alike. What we cannot do is escape each other, no matter the gothic-horror potential of relationships.[50]

One Sunday at Community Christian Church in Naperville, Illinois, the worship leader walked to the center of the auditorium and asked the audience to turn and face him. He then asked the audience to look at the faces of the people around them. After a moment he said, "When we turn our eyes upon Jesus, we are turning our eyes upon the church and each other." They then sang the hymn "Turn Your Eyes upon Jesus."

Turn your eyes upon Jesus,
Look full in his wonderful face,
And the things of earth will grow
    strangely dim
In the light of his glory and grace.[52]

We contain the other, hopelessly and forever.

Novelist/essayist
James Baldwin

Normal people create relationships that keep "others" out. NUTS relationships find ways to bring "others" in. NUTS disciples never withhold love from anyone.

Jesus found ways to be with "others," "with" these "other" kinds of people, in incarnational ways. He modeled a "with-without" pathway."[53] With them in love and care, without judgment. With them in encouragement and comfort, without condition. With them in support and healing, without self concern. NUTS ministry follows this with-without pathway.

The Brazil Nut Effect

Shake a can of mixed nuts long enough, and the biggest nuts end up on top. This is called the Brazil Nut Effect. Why? It used to be thought that the big guys rise because the smaller nuts in a shaking container fill in the gaps that open beneath the larger nuts.

This is only a part of the explanation. Recent research has discovered that when a cylinder is shaken, a convective flow ensues in which particles rise at the middle and fall at the sides. It's this churning that lands the big nuts at the top. Particle density has a part to play in this process as well, since heavier nuts rise faster than lighter ones even when they're of the same size.

But most recently, researchers were surprised to find that at normal pressure the race to the top is won by both the heaviest and the lightest nuts. The more abnormal the pressure—the more air pulled out of the canister—the more equal everyone becomes during the shaking. Size and weight matter less and less until, in an evacuated cylinder being shaken, a nut of almost any weight or size rises faster than it would in normal pressure.[54]

In other words, take away normal air pressure, and any size can rise to the top. Air affects the movement of even the smallest particles.

This is what NUTS people do. NUTS people take away "normal" air pressure so that anyone can rise to the top.

Anyone and everyone. ALL races, all classes, all nationalities, but especially the small of the all—those whom society marginalizes and despises. For Christians who are NUTS, the periphery becomes the center.

Mixed NUTS

The church is a nuthouse, but it is packed with mixed nuts, not just one kind. The HUP (homogenous unit principle) method of separating nuts by kind and variety violates the withness of Christian spirituality. Name one church in the New Testament that isn't multicultural. There is no Acts 2 church without mixed NUTS. NUTS disciples have no interest in looking in a mirror when they worship.

Mixed NUTS, yes. But *not* "Deluxe Mixed NUTS." *Only* "Regular Mixed NUTS." Whenever you see that word "deluxe," you know that the lowly peanut has been expunged from the midst. For NUTS disciples, those vulgar, common, no-good peanuts have got to be there. I know. I'm one of them—a goober for God.

At the 16th annual induction ceremony for the Rock and Roll Hall of Fame in 2001, U2's Bono looked out at the crowd and announced, "The whole world is full of freaks. . . . Look at yourselves! God makes music out of his mistakes. I know—I'm one of them."[55]

When the church stops looking out for the little guys or caring for the bottom of the human heap or specializing in the forgotten, the freaks, and the mistakes, it has ceased being the church. St. Cyprian, the third-century Bishop of Carthage in North Africa, quoted Jesus as saying, "It is in yourselves that you see me, just as a man looking in a mirror will see his own reflection."

Can you see the face of Jesus in the peanuts of the poor?

Can you see the face of Jesus in the peanuts of the imprisoned?

Can you see it in the peanuts of the oppressed?

Can you see it in the peanuts of the homeless?

Can you see it in the peanuts of the down and out?

Can you see it in the peanuts of the up and out?

Have you ever noticed how those who claim to love the peanuts the most get involved the least? The governor of Mississippi once challenged each of the state's 5,500 churches and synagogues to help one poor family to get back on its feet. That's all—just take on one family. Only 267 took up the challenge. Within a few years, when they checked back, a mere 15 churches were still doing it and were matched with families.[56] Evangelical Christians are "significantly less likely than are non-Christians to give money for AIDS education and prevention programs worldwide."[57] How often are Christians noted for their courageous defense of unpopular causes?

The Witness of Your Withness

One way of measuring the witness of your withness is to use the evaluation tool that Thomas Aquinas developed to analyze beauty, especially the perfect beauty of the Trinity. True beauty (in our case, the beauty of a NUTS witness) can be gauged by a trio of qualities: wholeness, harmony, and radiance.

1. Wholeness refers to pure existence itself. Are you "with it"? Is your being paying attention to the withness of life? Wholeness is the intention of attention.

It is not easy to be "with it." In fact, some are calling this the "attention economy" because the scarcest commodity today is "attention." It is especially not easy to pay attention to what people are going through and the connections that bind them to what you're going through. Simone Weil believed that "the capacity to give one's attention to a sufferer is a very rare and difficult thing: it is almost a miracle; it *is* a miracle." Weil loved the story of Percival/Parsifal, the only knight to attain the Grail because he was the only one to turn aside when it was within his grasp and ask its suffering guardian, "What are you going through?"

Preacher Ted Haggard offers a definition of discipleship that has as its "fundamental theorem" a "withness" formula: "discipleship = relationship + intentionality."[58] In other words, true discipleship is intentional attention, the purposeful "being with" each other.

The witness of wholeness is an openness to the distress signals of the self, other people, and planet Earth. NUTS disciples not only bother about, but get bothered by what is going on in the wider world.

2. Harmony means a respect and resonance for the relationships between things. When any relationship is off-key or disharmonious, when anyone scrapes against another, everyone's relationships are compromised. In a world where everyone is connected, we carry each other or we get carried away. Like Atlas, each of us carries the universe on our shoulders. Every move I make, every direction I take, shakes and tilts the whole cosmos on its axis. But unlike Atlas, we don't have to carry the weight of the universe on our shoulders alone. We carry it together. But drop the ball, and the whole planet becomes a basket case.

Poverty is one of the biggest killers of humanity. When one-third of the earth's population is imprisoned in poverty, it is easy for the two-thirds not in poverty to be seen as the jailers. A world in which 10% of the people are enormously wealthy and 50% are exceedingly poor is a very volatile place. Jesus put it like this: Care for the poor, or go to hell.

The withness of harmony is living a life that brings relationships back into harmony, that helps others get "with it" in lives of range and resonance without fusing faith and any social ethics option. One study makes the case that $27 billion could save 8 million lives a year. If every citizen in a rich country would give $25 per year extra, 8 million lives a year could be saved.[60] That's all it takes to ease tremendous suffering and anguish—less than 50 cents a week. Billions of people are crying for my help. Instead of hearing their cries, I close my ears and go merrily on my shopping sprees for stocking stuffers, purchasing Martha's latest ladle or Eddie Bauer's best buckskin jacket. Is something wrong here?

> *The U.S. has built a humongous mansion in the middle of a world with a lot of slums.*
>
> Kenyan entrepreneur Ayisi Makatiani, founder, Africa Online[59]

The early Celtic teacher Pelagius got a lot wrong in his theology, but one of the things he got right was his insistence that love does not merely stop us from doing certain things. More important, he said, is that love starts us on paths of service and justice. "I do not wish you to suppose that righteousness consists simply in not doing evil, since not to do good is also evil," Pelagius said. "Indeed, you are instructed . . . not only not to take bread away from one who has it but willingly to bestow your own on one who has none."[61] It is not enough that we're not causing poverty. The witness of harmony instills in us a desire to share what we have to alleviate poverty.

The harmony of withness does not separate spiritual realities from material realities like racial reconciliation and social justice. The sin of Dives in the Bible? He thinks he has five brothers. He actually has six: the homeless and the poor are his sixth.[62] In fact, on this basis we will be judged on the last day, when Jesus himself will ask, "Was I hungry and you gave me no food, was I thirsty and you gave me nothing to drink, was I a stranger and you did not welcome me?"[63]

It is not enough just to look up. If we are to escape the foul smells of eternity, the withness of harmony requires us to show up for those whose lives are dissonant and deprived, those with "withnesses" that spontaneously combust.

3. The witness of radiance is the clarity of our intelligibility and communication. If we look up (wholeness) and show up (harmony), we must also speak up and speak out (radiance). Radiant mystery is another name for the gospel of Jesus Christ.

When we take the most absorbing and mysterious story in history and turn it into a dull diatribe, radiance is ruined. Is our withness crisp and convincing? How transparent is our truthfulness? As we have seen, the clear-sighted often appears cock-eyed to the world. So the question is better stated, how can we communicate our craziness better?

> **I believe that if a person can't communicate, the very least he can do is to shut up!**
>
> Humorist
> Tom Lehrer

Radiance is made manifest more in flesh than in utterance. Why not invite people to join us in our craziness? We can ask them to be "with" us when we go to the movies and go out later to reflect on what we saw. We can ask people to be "with" us when we visit people in jail or in the hospital. Instead of creating "I" relationships, the witness of radiance creates "we" relationships around which we form "with" rituals. Using Jesus' "with-me" principle, deep relationships develop in which we can communicate most powerfully the witness of our withness.

The homeland of radiance is hope. Hopelessness has no homeland, but it is not homeless. It is "at home" in the tiniest corner of discontent and disconnect. The withness of radiance is a life that never loses hope. A great deal of our clumsiness in communicating the gospel is a direct result of our wilting expectations and dispiriting dreams when faced with devilishly difficult problems. Some time ago William Raspberry wrote a column entitled "When Social Conscience Gives Way to Despair." It described something that each one of us has experienced.

There is no better mirror than an old friend.
Old Japanese proverb

Raspberry recited the problem of homelessness and the multitude of reasons for the homeless on our streets: the deinstitutionalization of the mentally ill, the reality that mentally ill people don't always take their medications and so become more mentally ill, the fact that government is less and less willing to provide social services and shelter, the low profit margins of low-cost urban housing. After a while, Raspberry confessed, his concern toppled like ninepins. "I no longer see homelessness as a problem that's likely to be solved anytime soon and, as a result, I find it hard to sustain much interest in it. . . . You don't have to be mean spirited to walk away from social problems. All it takes is the certainty that nothing can be done to solve them."[64]

At the first puff of real wind, does our hope disappear into the thin, low-pressure air of despair?

Because Jesus stretched the category of hope at the seams, hope swells in the craziest of stitches.

"Absolutely Nutty": ALL

Who in the rainbow can draw the line where the violet tint ends and the orange tint begins? Distinctly we see the difference of the colors, but where exactly does the one first blendingly enter into the other? So with sanity and insanity.

—Herman Melville[1]

A little boy was walking with his father through a parking lot one day. He looked at a puddle that had formed and said, "Look, Daddy, there's a rainbow that has gone to smash."

The two words don't seem to go together: smash and rainbow. The rainbow has become a sort of visual shorthand for an arch of promise and peace. The Illinois state lottery logo is a pot of gold at the end of a rainbow. Another Illinois entity, "The Rainbow Coalition," uses the rainbow as a mobilizing symbol for racial justice.

Once again we have managed to mangle and trivialize a biblical symbol. The rainbow is not given to us as a symbol of hope or as a reminder to us of God's faithfulness or even as a symbol of peace. The rainbow is God's symbol: it was put in the sky to remind God of the covenant God made with humanity and with creation.[2] Circumcision or baptism is *our* reminder of God's covenant. The rainbow is God's reminder of the divine covenant with humanity: whenever God looked out and saw it, God's disgust with our ways would not lead to cursing creation back into oblivion.

The rainbow is the safety lock behind God's trigger finger.

In fact, when rainbows necklace the sky in Christian art, it is often to portray Christ in majesty, who customarily sits on a rainbow or two as he passes final judgment on humanity. As in other ancient cultures, the rainbow can be a menacing or ominous symbol.[3] That is why many cultures made it a taboo to point at the rainbow or even to look at it. In fact, to "break a rainbow" was a serious offense and could stir up evil in your life.

Yet rainbows that break are a part of what it means to be human. Like Robin Williams, who confesses that his comedy "steers between rainbows and cesspools,"[4] life has a way of turning rainbows into cesspools. Anyone reading this not an authority on smashed rainbows? Anyone out there who hasn't had your hopes and dreams smashed until you're stumbling about in the dark—smashed by financial reverses, health issues, professional failures, marital stress, family problems?

Has anyone not been crushed by life until you can't see straight: crushed in your character, your physical health, your spiritual life, your job, your marriage? Crushed by ungrateful and demanding children, by personal battles with lust and anger, by pile-ups that bog-down, by the collapse of two gleaming towers that mirrored the sky and reflected our feelings of superiority?

The writer of Ecclesiastes looked around, saw lives ruined by cruel twists of fate, and offered advanced courses in smashed rainbows: "In this meaningless life of mine I have seen both of these: a righteous man perishing in his righteousness, and a wicked man living long in his wickedness."[5]

The Psalmist knew a smashed rainbow when he saw one: "This is what the wicked are like—always carefree, they increase in wealth. Surely in vain have I kept my heart pure; in vain have I washed my hands in innocence."[6]

Job, who of all people knew how life can leave you shipwrecked through no fault of your own, used a smashed rainbow to haul in the only lifeboat available: "Why do the wicked live on, growing old and increasing in power?"[7]

John the gospel writer predicted you can't escape the pressures that press life's rainbows out of shape. He said, "In the world you have tribulation."[8] The Greek word *thlypsis,* often translated "tribulation," just as readily means "pressure."

Even Jesus knew a smashed rainbow: "My God, my God, why have you forsaken me?"[9]

Do you think you've seen the last of them? Do you think life gets simpler or easier the more life runs down? "Why do new waves of trouble keep pounding around me/before yesterday's waves ebb away?" Dan Foster asks in his song "There's a Reason." The marks of passing time—liver spots, love handles, crows' feet, senior moments, body barnacles—do you want me to continue spelling out the body's mutinous ways? The awful truth is this: at the end of life, things can fall apart just as easily as fall into place.

> Wherever we turn our eyes, there is God's symbol.
>
> Ephrem the Syrian (fourth century)

In the movie *Before and After* (1996), the narrator, a young girl, says, "Your whole world can change in a second and you never even know when it's coming. Before, you think you know what kind of a world this is, and after, everything is different for you ... forever. I didn't used to know that, till the day it happened to my family. I didn't even know there could be such a thing as after. I didn't know that for us, before was already over."[10]

A person's whole life can change in an instant. Life can go dead in a second. In Alice Hoffman's novel *At Risk*, there is a character, Polly Farrell, who says, "Everything too terrible to imagine suddenly happens, it happens when your back is turned, just when you think everything is fine."[11]

> Is there a 'before and after' in your life?
> If not now, there will be.
> Before and After an
> > unforeseen danger
> > unanticipated accident
> > unwanted arrival
> > sudden twist of wind
> > shocking directive
> > staggering loss

Do you know what to do when you're hanging on by your fingernails, feeling scattered and battered? Do you know how to get on with life after an "after"? Do you know the secret to smashed rainbows?

There is one.

> *All things . . . are charged with love,*
> *are charged with God, and if we know how*
> *to touch them give off sparks and take fire,*
> *yield drops and flow, ring and tell of him.*
>
> Poet Gerard Manley Hopkins[12]

To be sure, there must be no sentimentality about smashed rainbows. "Too long a sacrifice can make a stone of the heart" is how W. B. Yeats put it.[13] But suffering can bring us closer to God and to each other. We experience more the power and love of God when rainbows smash than when they shine.

The Secret

The apostle Paul, while in prison awaiting death, said he learned the "secret" of smashed rainbows. What's the secret—the secret of "being content" in any and every situation,[14] the secret wherewithall to endure all smashed rainbows?

Paul's secret is this: "I can do *all* things through [Christ] who strengthens me."[15]

The secret is the three-letter word *all*. A secret so simple, yet so complex, so mysterious. "For mortals it is impossible, but not for God; for God all things are possible."[16] If you are Christ's, "all things are yours."[17] God wants to do in your life "above all that we ask or think,"[18] and God will supply "all your need."[19]

Because of this *all* word, God adds an apostrophe and an opening to that word *impossible:* "I'm possible." When the rainbow is most smashed is when your life can most come together, when God is at work in you and perfecting the divine energy in you.

> *There will come a time when you believe that everything is finished. That will be the beginning.*
>
> Novelist Louis L'Amour

If Ursula LeGuin is right that the little words make the biggest difference, this three-letter word *all* is the secret to smashed rainbows.

> Jesus paid it all,
> All to Him I owe;
> Sin had left a crimson stain,
> He washed it white as snow.[20]

All is the crimson tip on the white cane that keeps us tapping forward into the dark. Stumbling over one smashed rainbow after another, it's that *all* that keeps us going.

Find me a hymn that doesn't have this red-tip *all* in it.

Praise God from Whom All Blessings Flow
Fight the Good Fight with All Your Might
For All the Saints
Let All Mortal Flesh Keep Silence
All Glory, Laud and Honor
All Hail the Power of Jesus' Name

The red-tip *all* is everywhere in the Bible. There are a lot of *all* promises. But before the crimson-tipped white cane can lead us forward when life blinds us, we need one more thing: a pacemaker.

A pacemaker regulates the heart when it is skipping beats and pulsing erratically. When the Word of God sinks into our souls and minds, there is a divine transplant of a pacemaker that governs the movement of our hearts so that even when we can't beat or speak on our own, the Word beats inside us.[21] Our pacemaker becomes a peacemaker for the "peace that passes all understanding."

"God shall wipe away all tears."
"Behold, I make all things new."
You "shall inherit all things."
"Quench all the flaming arrows."
The blood of Christ "cleanses us from
  all sin" and "from all unrighteousness."
God wants to "make known to you all things."[22]

This three-letter word transforms whatever your manse into a mansion, whatever your Sheol into a Shiloh. Because of this word, we can praise God for every side of life—for friends, lovers, art, literature, knowledge, humor, politics—and the little red cloud away there in the West.

But all the *all* promises cling like Krazy Glue to this one verse: Is Christ your "all and in all"?[23] When Paul talks about God being "all in all," he recognizes that God is already "all." It is our ministry to put God "in all" so that "all things are subjected to him" and he will be "all in all."[24] Is it your prayer "that God may be all in all"?

One of the worst sentences a Christian could receive in the days of the Roman persecution was to be sent to the mines of Numidia in North Africa. Rather than immediate death by being eaten by lions or burned at the stake, death was slow and indescribable, through brutal whippings, charbroiling under the sun, hot-iron brandings that became infected and gangrenous, exhaustion in dark mines, accidents in rocky valleys.

When the mines of Numidia were opened up to visitors, it was discovered that these early Christians had etched little words and slogans on the walls of the caves in which they were working. Of all the many words that appear there, two appear more than any others: *Christ* (*Christos*) and *life*.

How crazy can you get?

All reminds us that God likes to appear in strange and unlikely places. *All* tips God's hand to the divine penchant for working in our lives and world in ways beyond our comprehension. Like Jacob's dream ladder, where angels were ascending and descending and God was speaking—"Know that I am with you and will keep you wherever you go"— we too awake from our sleep and say like Jacob, "Surely the LORD is in this place—and I did not know it!"[25]

You know how much you love and care for your kids. You want to give them everything that is good for them. Do you think God would treat you, a child of his, worse than you, a parent, would treat your own children?

God's possibilities are endless. NUTS disciples dream big. Little dreams have no magic. The crisis of faith today has more to do with the imagination than with the intellect. The Greek myth of Prometheus had humans stealing fire from the gods and being punished for it. In the Christian tradition, God gave humans the fire and rewards humanity for exercising its call to dream—to be creative and continue his creativity by dreaming his dream for the world.

Jesus calls us to refuse to accept life on the terms offered us by smashed rainbows. We are not called to make our own terms with life. We are called to make God's terms with life.

Our world is full of lost souls whose limitations have become their limits.

We have conquered the atom, yet too many are atomized by greed and selfishness.

We have conquered DNA, yet too many are predestined by their insatiable appetites.

We have conquered the moon, yet too many are enslaved by earthbound fixations.

We have conquered outer space, yet too many are lost in the emptiness of their inner space.

Freedom is not the absence of limitations. True freedom is acknowledging your limitations and connecting your limitations to God's limitless *all*. Complete freedom is the end of freedom, but the Spirit makes us more free by helping us work within limitations as finite, contingent creatures who lean on an infinite, boundless God. In the spiritual sphere as in the political sphere, it is wise restraints that make us free; our limitations make us rely on the God Beyond *All* Limits.

The only way you can have it all is if you realize you can't have it all. You can only have all that you are willing to sacrifice for, value most, pay the cost for, counting "all things but loss."[26]

If I had known what it would be like to have it all, I might have settled for less.

Humorist Lily Tomlin

Søren Kierkegaard wrote that the strangest thing ever said about love was "to a certain degree." Love with all or don't love at all. How did Jesus put it? "Love the Lord your God with all your heart, with all your soul, and with all your strength, and with all your mind."[27]

My favorite line in Elvis Presley's song "Big Hunk of Love" is "I ain't greedy, Baby, all I want is all you got!" All God wants is all you got. Nothing more, nothing less.

The Law

The phrase "the Law of Christ" is used two times in the New Testament.[28] What is "the law of Christ"?

Love.

When as Christians we say, "It's the law," what "law" are we talking about?

Love.

> **Better no love than love, which, through loving Leads to no love.**
>
> Irish poet Denis Devlin[29]

It's the law: The law of Christ is love. What is Jesus' farewell commandment? "Love one another as I have loved you."[30]

The law of Christ is a love that comes from "the God of all comfort,"[31] a love that lasts, that "bears all things, believes all things, hopes all things, endures all things."[32]

A love that bears all things

- Bears burdens to bless others: my burden, your blessing
- Bears fruit even from lost causes, last chances, and long shots
- Grins and bears all because when your back is up against the wall, your face is up against the cross

Whether "living in the teeth of death" (as Martin Luther put it) or staring death in the face, "Christians above all are those who should be able to bear reality and show others how to bear it."[33]

A love that believes all things

- Believes that Jesus can change human nature into God's nature
- Believes God's "immortal spirit is in all things"[34]
- Believes if we call upon God, he "will answer you, and I will tell you great and mighty things, which you do not know"[35]
- Believes in making rainbows in a world where people are working hard to shatter rainbows—raining down hatred, bombs, and threats of nuclear rain
- Believes in the right of everyone to be free from poverty and exploitation
- Believes that "from him and through him and to him are all things"[36] and that "he himself is before all things, and in him all things hold together. . . . For in him all the fullness of God was pleased to dwell, and through him God was pleased to reconcile to himself all things, whether on earth or in heaven, by making peace through the blood of his cross"[37]

A love that hopes all things

- Hopes that your disabled child, whose brain has been freeze-framed by encephalitis, can "take hold of the life that is truly life"[38]
- Hopes that your church will be a place "where the GED's and Ph.D.'s can sit down together, play together, and worship together" (as Brian McLaren puts it)

A love that endures all things[39]

- Endures with uncomplaining graciousness the strokes of a spouse who is now incapacitated and incontinent: "Love is not love/Which alters when alteration finds."[40]
- Endures and endures and will "never give up. Though our bodies are dying, our inner strength in the Lord is growing every day."[41]

Love Crazy

This kind of *all* love is a love the world calls *crazy* and a love that drives you *crazy*.[42] Jesus, the greatest Lover the world has ever known, drove people crazy with this kind of outrageous love. His unquenchable and unconsidered love was scandalous. Jesus' love constantly pushed the outrage envelope. And he called his disciples to continue what he started and themselves become the greatest lovers the world has ever known.

Jesus came to tell us we have a God who is crazy in love with us.

This love is sheer madness. Do you wonder that some people thought he was certifiable?

Jesus' relatives once sought to end his public ministry on the grounds that he was mentally deranged. They thought he was absolutely nutty because people were saying that Jesus had "gone out of his mind."[43]

Procurator Festus told Paul his gospel was "madness." This time Paul defended himself. "I am not crazy, most excellent Festus. What I am saying is true and reasonable."[44]

Later Paul admitted he was certifiable. He said, "Whether we went mad, [it was] for God; or whether we are in our right mind, [it is] for you."[45] In other words: I really *am* crazy. God has driven me NUTS. But I'm holding on to sanity because of you and my need to communicate the truth to you. Otherwise I'd be even crazier than I am.

This verse intrigued Augustine, who refers to it several times. Some scholars try to explain away this passage by saying it refers to Paul's language, not his life.[46] Some commentators wipe their hands of ever understanding these verses.[47] Other scholars call the passage "Paul's self-portrait." It's a passage I believe should be every disciple's self-portrait.

Paul is contrasting here being *existemi* ("out of mind") and *sophoneo* ("in one's right mind"). He uses *sophoneo* one other time to describe reasoned, purposive, controlled, sober, appropriate behavior.[49]

> *It is strange how the world considers a man unbalanced when his life is fully consecrated to the Lord.*
> Wick Broomall[48]

All scholars agree that these two verbs remain opposites. But what the opposites refer to is hotly debated. Most say Paul is opposing the ecstatic experiences for which he is well-known (such as visions, tongues, obscure teachings about seventh heavens, out-of-control behavior) with rational, judicious conduct.[50] But I am convinced that Paul is opposing being "outrageous" and sometimes "beside himself" with being "together" and "controlled." Why is Paul sometimes "beside himself"? Because the love of Christ drives him crazy. Love is the controlling force in his life. He does try to behave in ways that edify others and show he's in his "right mind," but the very thing that "constrains" him for the sake of not putting off others is the very thing that drives him crazy: the love of Christ.

Paul is really saying here, "I'm both. I can present myself as the paragon of reasoned argument and speech, but when I'm not trying to pass myself off as something I'm truly not for your sake, I confess: I'm mental. Jesus' love has driven me crazy."

Are you certifiable?

Are you getting that "I'm-with-a-crazy-person" look or shrug?

Every major advance in church history was made by crazies—Martin Luther, Philip Melanchthon, John Calvin, John Wesley, Daniel Zwicker, William and Catherine Booth, Charles G. and Elizabeth Atkinson Finney, Hudson Taylor, Phoebe Palmer, Martin Luther King Jr., Mother Teresa.

A half century ago, a British lawyer had an idea only a few took seriously: when repressive governments take innocent citizens prisoner, flood them with letters and telegrams of protest. This idea was quickly and widely characterized as "one of the larger lunacies of our time,"[51] and its originator, Peter Benenson, was ridiculed and attacked with the force of a sledgehammer on nuts.

> **To be odd in the world is God's intention for his people.**
>
> Biblical scholar
> Walter Brueggemann

So began Amnesty International.[52] Now AI has supporters in more than 160 countries and a budget of 19.5 million pounds, and what began as "one man's lunacy" now is one world's conscience and one of the most respected NGO's on the planet.

I admit it: I'm certifiable. I'm certifiably LoveCrazy. I'm madly in love with the Lover of Nazareth.

I believe in pointing that crimson-tipped cane and casting *"all* your anxiety on him, because he cares for you."[53] I'm LoveCrazy.

I believe in pointing that crimson-tipped cane and praying "in the Spirit on *all* occasions with *all* kinds of prayers and requests . . . always keep on praying for *all* the saints."[54] I'm LoveCrazy.

I believe in pointing that crimson-tipped cane till I find the "peace of God, which surpasses *all* understanding."[55] I'm LoveCrazy.

The central doctrine of the cross, "Christ for all: all in Christ," is the negation of selfishness, the affirmation of Jesus' law of love.[56] Urban monk Shane Claiborne, a founder of "The Simple Way" community in Philadelphia, shared with a group of Drew students his incomprehension of those who testify, "My life was a mess. I was all screwed up and then I met Jesus and my life came together." In his case, Shane says, it as exactly the opposite. "I had my life all together. I was on an upward track and heading toward medical school. Then I met Jesus, and he messed up my whole life."

A Canadian friend told me in an e-mail of this experience:

At our Vacation Bible School we used some rockin', stompin' new music but also went back to some of the moldy oldies. A favorite of the kids is always "Hallelu, hallelu, hallelu, hallelujah, Praise ye the Lord." It ain't the words the kids love as much as being able to bellow at the top of their lungs in a circus tent out back of the church.

Sang it once, kids loved it. "More, more, again, again." Sang it again. "One more time." Sang it again!

Next day a red-headed bundle of five-year-old perpetual motion asked if we could sing that song again.

"What song?" smiles me.

Carrot-top says, "Crazy the Lord."

"Crazy the Lord," I quizzically reply. "We never sang one like that!"

"Sure we did," says the hellion, looking at me like I've got mustard on the end of my nose. "Hallelu, hallelu, hallelu, hallelujah, crazy the Lord!"

I grinned the grin of one who knows they've just been blessed with the wisest bit of truth they'll hear for months, maybe years. Of course I didn't tell him what the real words were. I liked his version a whole lot more.

Crazy the Lord? Absolutely. Crazy for caring, crazy for loving, crazy for having anything whatsoever to do with us most-times pathetically self-centered, fumble-mouthed human beings.

Hallelu, hallelu, hallelu, hallelujah, crazy the Lord! Red was right. Crazy indeed.

> *A man needs a little madness or else*
> *he never dares to cut the rope and be free.*
>
> Novelist Nikos Kazantzakis[57]

The most dangerous person in the world? It's not a terrorist like Osama bin Laden. It's the person who terrorizes normality with the love crazy power of these three letters: a-l-l.

Call me crazy, but I'm still crazy enough to believe that

> Jesus loves me, this I know
> For the Bible tells me so.[58]

Call me crazy, but I'm still crazy enough to believe that

> The B-I-B-L-E,
> Yes, that's the Book for me.

Call me crazy, but I still believe that

> What can wash away my sin?
> Nothing but the blood of Jesus.[59]

Call me crazy, but I still believe that

> Jesus is the sweetest name I know.[60]

Call me crazy, but I still believe that

> I've got a home in glory land that outshines the sun.

Call me crazy, but I still believe that

> I've got the joy, joy, joy, joy down in my heart.

Call me crazy, but I still believe that

> Because He lives, I can face tomorrow.[61]

Call me crazy, but I still believe that

> Be not dismayed whate'er betide,
> God will take care of you.[62]

Call me crazy, but I still believe that

> Soon and very soon
> We're goin to see the King.[63]

Call me crazy, but I still believe that

> Surely, the presence of the Lord is in this place.[64]

Call me crazy, but I still believe that

> My hope is built on nothing less. . . .
> All other ground is sinking sand.[65]

Or how has Billy Graham been driving us NUTS for 50 years? When life blinds us by smashed rainbows, or we're stumbling about in the dark, is our pacemaker beating out the rhythm . . .

> Just as I am, poor, wretched, blind—
> Sight, riches, healing of the mind,
> Yea, all I need in Thee to find—
> O Lamb of God, I come![66]

The recovery of NUTS wisdom in Christian discipleship is part of the healing of the world.

When the tribe of Jesus lives out its crazy wisdom in the world and rightly "breaks" the "Bread of Life" for all to eat, the world will truly "find [its] Peace, [its] All in All."[67]

Are you wise enough to be crazy?

Notes

Introduction

1. Herman Melville, *Moby Dick, or The Whale* (Garden City, NY: Garden City Publishing, 1937), 599 (ch. 93).
2. In Alcoholics Anonymous, those outside the group are called "normies." See Warehouse 242, "Our Mission," www.warehouse242.org. Accessed 3 February 2002.
3. Edwin Muir, "The Incarnate One," from his *One Foot in Eden* (1956), reprinted in *The Complete Poems of Edwin Muir: An Annotated Edition*, ed. Peter Butter (Aberdeen: The Association for Scottish Literary Studies, 1991), 213.
4. Jimmy Carter, *An Hour before Daylight: Memoirs of a Rural Boyhood* (New York: Simon & Schuster, 2001), 266.
5. The Christ metanarrative is the comprehensive story that shapes our total being in Christ—who we are, what we believe, what we aspire to become. See the section on "The Ecclesial Self as Narrative" in Stanley J. Grenz, *The Social God and the Relational Self: A Trinitarian Theology of the Imago Dei* (Louisville: Westminster John Knox Press, 2001), 328–31.
6. 2 Corinthians 5:16.
7. Thomas V. Morris, "Suspicions of Something More" in *God and the Philosophers: The Reconciliation of Faith and Reason*, ed. Thomas V. Morris (New York: Oxford University Press, 1994), 8–9.
8. In the doctrine of the incarnation, the way up, toward the stars of heaven, is down, toward what the ancient Celts called "the stars within the earth."
9. John 13:3–5.
10. Remember the words "Hold o'er my being absolute sway" from Adelaide A. Pollard's "Have Thine Own Way, Lord," *The*

United Methodist Hymnal: Book of United Methodist Worship
(Nashville: United Methodist Publishing House, 1989), 382.

11. Ecclesiasticus, or the Wisdom of Jesus Son of Sirach 10:28 RSV.

12. Barbara Brown Taylor, *Bread of Angels* (Cambridge, MA:
Cowley, 1997), 125, 124.

13. Julie Gibbs, "At the Helm: Larry Ellison," *Oracle Magazine*
(January/February 2002): 58. www.oracle.com/oramag/oracle/
02-jan/index.html?o12larry.html. Accessed 2 May 2002.

14. Matthew 20:28. "Jesus, knowing that the Father had given all
things into his hands, and that he had come from God and
was going to God, got up from the table, took off his outer
robe, and tied a towel around himself. Then he poured water
into a basin and began to wash the disciples' feet and to wipe
them with the towel that was tied around him" (John 13:3–5).

15. "The Spirit of him who raised Jesus from the dead is living in
you" (Romans 8:11 NIV).

16. *Enthusiasm* comes from the Greek word meaning "God
within."

17. There was an ancient Greek saying, "A people are known by
the heroes they crown." A hero is half human and half divine,
said the Greeks. Christians claimed Jesus was more than a
hero: He was fully human and fully divine.

18. John 1:11. Some of the saddest words of Scripture are these:
"He was in the world, and the world came into being through
him; yet the world did not know him" (John 1:10).

19. "I, when I am lifted up from the earth, will draw all people to
myself" (John 12:32).

20. *The Apology of Aristides the Philosopher,* trans. from the
Syriac by D. M. Kay, in *The Ante-Nicene Fathers: Translations
of the Writings of the Fathers Down to A.D. 325,* ed. Allan
Menzies, 5th ed. (New York: Charles Scribner's Sons, 1906),
9:277–78. www.earlychristianwritings.com/text/aristides-
kay.html. Accessed February 2003.

21. My Presbyterian colleague and friend Dan Anderson-Little
says about ministry in the church, "I don't mind being a 'thorn
in the flesh,' but I sure don't like being a thorn in the corpse."

22. Keith Griswold suggests an alternative rendering of NUTS:
Now Under The Spirit.

23. Romans 5:6 NIV.

24. 1 Samuel 16:7c.

25. 1 Samuel 16:7d.

26. Old Latin translation of Isaiah 7:9.

27. Bruce Cockburn, "The Trouble with Normal," The Cockburn Project: Bruce Cockburn online: www.cockburnproject.net/ frames.html. Accessed 3 February 2002.

28. Luke 10:21.

29. Matthew 18:3–4.

30. 2 Corinthians 12:9–10.

31. Isaiah 53:2 NIV.

32. Augustine, "Sermon 27," in *The Works of Saint Augustine, A Translation for the 21st Century: Sermons* (Brooklyn: New City Press, 1990), 3/2:107.

33. Ezekiel 22:26.

34. Revelation 3:16 NRSV.

35. For more see Philip Zaleski, "Holy Folly: Three Foolish Ways to Find God," *Parabola* 26 (Fall 2001): 28.

36. Charles Wesley, "Awake Thou That Sleepest," in John Wesley, *Sermons*, ed. Albert C. Outler, vol. 1 of *The Works of John Wesley* (Nashville: Abingdon Press, 1984), 1:156. Preached on Sunday, April 4, 1742, before the University of Oxford.

37. See Nan Runde, "At Home in the Land of the Little Green Waiting-Maid," *Parabola* 26 (Fall 2001): 27, note 1.

38. 2 Corinthians 12:11.

39. 1 Corinthians 3:18–19.

40. 1 Corinthians 4:9–10.

41. 1 Corinthians 1:27–29.

42. Andrew Stark, "The First Dead Parrot Sketch," *TLS: Times Literary Supplement*, 31 August 2001, 7.

43. Quoted in Beatrice K. Otto, *Fools Are Everywhere: The Court Jester around the World* (Chicago: University of Chicago Press, 2001), 112–13.

44. My gratitude goes to Eugene Peterson in *The Message* for correctly conveying the power of the word *moros*.

45. 1 John 4:19.

46. President John F. Kennedy, quoting Pierre Mendes France, quoting Charles de Gaulle as found in Eric Roussel, *Charles de Gaulle* (Paris: Gallimard, 2002).

47. Irish Jesuit William Johnston argues that the uniqueness of Christianity lies in "the belief that the Ultimate and Unutterable Mystery is BEING-IN-LOVE." See William Johnston, *"Arise, My Love": Mysticism for a New Era* (Maryknoll, NY: Orbis Books, 2000), 148.

48. *Catherine of Siena: The Dialogue,* trans. Suzanne Noffke, *The Classics of Western Spirituality* (New York: Paulist Press, 1980), 325.

49. See 1 Corinthians 2:1–5.

50. The expression "730" is street slang for crazy. It originated with the New York State Criminal Procedure Article 730, which sets the criteria for determining whether defendants are sane enough to stand trial.

51. Frederick Buechner, *The Life of Jesus* (New York: Weathervane Books, 1974), 136.

52. "Our starting question—why should there be madness in the human species?—has found an answer—because the traits that underlie madness are also beneficial for creativity" (Daniel Nettle, *Strong Imagination: Madness, Creativity and Human Nature* [New York: Oxford University Press, 2001], 168).

53. Theseus in William Shakespeare, *A Midsummer Night's Dream,* act 5, scene 1, lines 7–8, in *The Complete Works of Shakespeare* (New York: Grolier, 1958), 297.

54. Ray Dolan, "Through Cells of Madness", *TLS: Times Literary Supplement,* 31 August 2001, 10.

55. Samuel P. Oliner and Pearl M. Oliner, *Altruistic Personality: Rescuers of Jews in Nazi Europe* (New York: Free Press, 1988), 2–4.

56. Oliner and Oliner, *Altruistic Personality,* 142–70. Some of the other key differences between "bystanders" and "rescuers":

    1) bystanders were more likely to have come from abusive homes; rescuers came from homes where parents talked to their children, reasoned with them, and introduced them to morals;

    2) rescuers had "models" of caring in their homes, parents and relatives who were "community volunteers" and "brothers' keepers";

    3) rescuers were exposed to more diverse individuals in their homes—people from different religions, races, social classes.

57. After the death of her husband, Margaret married George Fox.

58. Ronald Rolheiser, OMI, "The Holy Longing/Seeking Spirituality," *Spirituality* 6 (March/April 2000): 123.

59. One of Peter Maurin's "Easy Essays," first published in the *Catholic Worker* (December 1935): as quoted in John C. Cort, "Crazy in His Own Way," *Catholic Worker* (May 1999): 3.

60. Adapted from "Are You Not Wanted?" author unknown, ed. Asa Sparks (shared by Carol), "Wit and Wisdom" (May 7 1998). www.sermonillustrator.org/areyou.htm. Accessed 11 January 2002.

Chapter One

1. Sun-Tzu, *The Art of War*, trans. Samuel B. Griffith (New York: Oxford University Press, 1977), 84.
2. Tina Sinatra with Jeff Coplon, *My Father's Daughter: A Memoir* (New York: Simon & Schuster, 2000), 45. Tina does not look at her father uncritically. Her conclusion about the Chairman of the Board is that "He was a man who all his life looked outside for what was missing inside" (22).
3. Richard H. Roberts, *Religion, Theology and the Human Sciences* (New York: Cambridge University Press, 2002), 114.
4. Ronald Blythe, *Divine Landscapes* (New York: Harcourt Brace Jovanovich, 1986), 127.
5. Jan Johnson, "Escaping the Christian Ghetto," published in the *M.B. Herald,* a newsletter of the Canadian Conference of Mennonite Brethren Churches. www.mbconf.ca/mb/mbh3521/ghetto.htm. Accessed 31 May 2002. With thanks to Andrew Careaga for this reference.
6. "Ingodded" is an Orthodox Christian phrase "used to describe someone who has given his life so totally unto God that he or she has become by Grace everything that God is by nature": as defined by Mark E. Cornelius in an Amazon.Com review of Alexander, Servant of God, *Father Arseny, 1893-1973: Priest, Prisoner, Spiritual Father* (Crestwood, NY: St. Vladmirs Seminary Press, 1998). www.amazon.com/exec/obidos/ ASIN/0881411809/103-9618290-9704621. Accessed 1 May 2002.

   For my own part, God's lesser attempts at artistic creation I call "bantam incarnations."
7. Character is an inside-out affair. Context is an outside-in dynamic. Yet, in some ways character and context do more than play off one another; they oppose one another. It's the state of relatedness between character and context that remains constant. For example, there is no one "right" way of doing church. Every strategy must be unique and relative to the specific relationships between the character of the church,

its leaders, and the specific context itself. The only thing constant is this relatedness, not the strategy.

8. Even those who attempt to escape incarnational "dating" can't. You had been able to order a butter churn from the Amish at their *amishgeneralstore.com* site. Inactive as of 6 June 2002.

9. 2 Chronicles 7:15–16 NIV.

10. Statistics quoted in Marcel Danesi, *Of Cigarettes, High Heels, and Other Interesting Things: An Introduction to Semiotics* (New York: St. Martin's Press, 1999), 48.

11. As quoted in Jonathan Alter, "Between the Lines: Hillary Raises Her Profile," *Newsweek*, 25 June 2001, 34.

12. See Ronald Rolheiser, *The Holy Longing: The Search for a Christian Spirituality* (New York: Doubleday, 1999), 102–3.

13. Oscar Wilde, "Phrases and Philosophies for the Use of the Young," *The Chameleon* 1 (December 1894): 1.

14. Isaiah 44:3–4 Living Bible.

15. The Moffatt translation of Romans 12:2.

16. I first gained this insight from columnist/humorist Jim Mullen, *It Takes a Village Idiot: Complicating the Simple Life* (New York: Simon & Schuster, 2001), 11.

17. Joseph L. Garlington, *Right or Reconciled? God's Heart for Reconciliation* (Shippensburg, PA: Destiny Image, 1998), 135.

18. William Blake, "To Thomas Butts," from "Selections from the Letters," in *The Portable Blake*, sel. and arr. by Alfred Kazin (New York: Penguin Books, 1946), 220.

19. William Blake, "Proverbs of Hell," in *The Marriage of Heaven and Hell,* in *The Portable Blake*, 254.

20. Fleming Rutledge, "Access to Power," in *Help My Unbelief* (Grand Rapids: Eerdmans, 2000), 57.

21. Marie Livingston Roy, as quoted in Ronald Rolheiser, *The Holy Longing: A Search for a Christian Spirituality* (New York: Doubleday, 1999), 101–2.

22. Within two years of Prozac's release into the market, 650,000 prescriptions were being written per month; in less than five years, over 8 million prescriptions were handed out. See Peter D. Kramer, *Listening to Prozac* (New York: Penguin Books, 1997), xvii, xix.

23. As quoted in David Macey, Introduction: "I, Michel Foucault," in his *The Lives of Michel Foucault: A Biography* (New York: Pantheon Books, 1993), xiii.

24. Isaiah 59:2.
25. James Hillman, *The Soul's Code: In Search of Character and Calling* (New York: Random House, 1996), 252.
26. Richard Sennett, *The Corrosion of Character: The Personal Consequences of Work in the New Capitalism* (New York: W. W. Norton, 1998), 10, 30.
27. e. e. cummings, as quoted in Charles Norman, *The Magic-Maker: E. E. Cummings* (New York: Macmillan, 1958), 384.
28. Galatians 4:19 NIV, italics mine.
29. Colossians 1:28 NIV, italics mine.
30. I first learned of this story from Cecily Boulding OP, in "Saints and Sinners on the Way to Calvary: Endurance," *Spirituality* (Dublin) 6 (March/April 2000): 94.
31. The lone dissent to this view comes from psychoanalyst Hans W. Loewald, who argued that it was through transference that the id becomes a mature and integrated ego. See Hans W. Loewald, *Psychoanalysis and the History of the Individual* (New Haven: Yale University Press, 1978), 22, or, for a fuller development, his *The Essential Loewald: Collected Papers and Monographs* (Hagerstown, MD: University Publishing Group, 2000).
32. Vicki León, *Uppity Women of Shakespearean Times* (New York: MJF Books, 1999), 259.
33. John 14:8–9.
34. For cheerfulness as a moral obligation ("Cheerlessness and moodiness are not victimless 'crimes'"), see Dennis Prager, *Happiness Is a Serious Problem: A Human Nature Repair Manual* (New York: ReganBooks, 1998).
35. Genesis 33:10.
36. See Exodus 34:29–30 and 2 Corinthians 3:7–11.
37. Matthew 17:2, 5; Luke 9:29.
38. 2 Corinthians 4:6.
39. 1 Corinthians 13:12.
40. Gregory of Nyssa, *The Life of Moses*, Classics of Western Spirituality (New York: Paulist Press, 1978), 114–15.
41. With thanks to colleague Frank Jeske for inspiring these thoughts.
42. Colossians 1:26–27.
43. As quoted by Basil Cardinal Hume, *The Mystery of the Incarnation* (Brewster, MA: Paraclete Press, 1999), 66.

44. Italo Calvino, quoting Gore Vidal's review of *If on a Winter's Night*, in his *Lettere 1940–1985,* ed. Luca Baranelli (Milan: Arnoldo Mondadori, 2001), 1242.

45. Meister Eckhart's sermon, "Sinking Eternally into God," in *Breakthrough: Meister Eckhart's Creation Spirituality in New Translation*, introduction and commentaries by Matthew Fox (Garden City, NY: Image Books, 1980), 179.

46. Barbara Jurgensen, *You're Out of Date, God?* (Grand Rapids: Zondervan, 1971), 57–59.

47. John 1:13.

48. I love how Parker T. Williamson puts it: "Nicene theology reminds us that we do not worship a mere idea. We worship a person. God was in Christ, reconciling the world to himself. Theologians who represent the Gospel as a system of thought miss the whole point" (Parker T. Williamson, *Standing Firm: Reclaiming Christian Faith in Times of Controversy* [Springfield, PA: PLC, 1996], 111).

49. Martin Luther, WA 40, II, 385.

50. Colossians 2:3.

51. As quoted in Tom Norris, "'You Have Loved Me, Therefore I Am!'" *Spirituality* 8 (January-February 2002): 27.

Chapter Two

1. Matthew 28:18–20.

2. Alistair McFadyen was the first to use this image of the person as being "sedimented" like layers of rock, with David Cunningham improving on the image through his suggestion of the "sediment" collected on a river-bed. See Alistair I. McFadyen, *The Call to Personhood: A Christian Theory of the Individual in Social Relationships* (New York: Cambridge University Press, 1990), 7–8, 72–73, and David S. Cunningham, *These Three Are One: The Practice of Trinitarian Theology* (Oxford: Blackwell, 1998), 199.

3. I thank Scotch Methodist Andrew Walls of St. Andrews, Scotland, for this connection between the "full stature of Christ" and cross-cultural incarnation. See his *The Cross-Cultural Process in Christian History: Studies in the Transmission and Appropriation of Faith* (Maryknoll, NY: Orbis Books, 2002), 77.

4. Wittgenstein taught that even the awareness that all knowledge is contextual does not mean that we can cavalierly shuck our own contexts. See his *On Certainty*, ed. G. E. M. Anscombe and G. H. Wright, trans. Denis Paul and G. E. M. Anscombe (New York: J. &. J. Harper, 1969).

5. 1 Corinthians 9:22.

6. Acts 19:28–41.

7. Three out of four members of an Irish rock band were Protestant Christians. When their sound began to take off, their spiritual leaders tried an intervention to "free" them from their emerging rock status. Miraculously, the members of the band freed themselves of this pressure without shedding their relationships with Jesus. The name of the group? U2.

8. Myla Goldberg, *Bee Season* (New York: Doubleday, 2000), 64.

9. Peter Slater, "Christ through Dialogue: Local and Global," *Sewanee Theological Review* 40 (1997): 405.

10. Connie Lauerman, "Turning Your Back on Doctors Orders: The Number of Patients Failing to Do What They're Told Is Reaching Epidemic Proportions," *Chicago Tribune*, NW Edition, 19 November 2000, 13:1.

11. The most comprehensive survey to date of American congregational pastors revealed a surprisingly high degree of satisfaction with their call to ministry but an equally surprisingly high degree of frustration with their ability to communicate the gospel in the current cultural context. See www.pulpitandpew.duke.edu. Accessed 1 June 2002.

12. "The Osbournes" is the biggest hit in the 24-year history of MTV. For a marvelous essay on Ozzy Osbourne and Alice Cooper, see Steve Beard, "The Way of Faith for Alice Cooper," at www.thunderstruck.org. Accessed 1 June 2002.

13. Alfred North Whitehead, *Adventures of Ideas* (New York: Macmillan, 1933), 41.

14. For more on EPIC, see my *Postmodern Pilgrims: First-Century Passion for the 21st-Century World* (Nashville: Broadman & Holman, 2000).

15. Quoted in Regina Fazio Koenigsberg, "State of the New Economy," *Fast Company* (September 2000): 106. www.fastcompany.com/online/38/one.html. Accessed 19 October 2001.

16. Peter Nelson, "Don't Mess with Me! Why Fight When You Can Just Look Scary?" *National Wildlife* (June-July 1994): 5.

17. David Sexton, *The Strange World of Thomas Harris* (London: Short Books, 2001), 12.

18. See www.cbe.wsu.edu/departments/hra/Bio.html. Accessed 12 October 2001.

19. See www.flash.stanford.edu/~horowitz/. Accessed 12 October 2001.

20. See catalog.arizona.edu/faculty/994/MKTG.html and www.be.wvu.edu/divmim/mktg/achrol/. Both accessed 13 January 2002.

21. The Parents Television Council (PTC) figures that only 12% of early prime-time series (the "family hour") are suitable for all ages. See Parents Television Council www.parentstv.org/.

22. At a taping of MTV's *Dude, This Sucks* (January 2001), the Shower Rangers were about to conclude their musical comedy when a member of the group turned his backside to the audience and defecated, splattering teenage spectators. Thankfully, the potty episode never aired, but there is plenty of airing of belching, farting, masturbating, breast-flashing, and people being lit on fire or doused with the contents of an outhouse to make up for it.

23. Read Mercer Schuchardt, "Play Boy! The Cultural Victory of Hugh Hefner," *re:generation* 7 (Fall 2001): 30. www.regenerator.com/7.3/schuchardt.html. Accessed 13 January 2002.

24. Cavafy, "The City," as quoted in Lawrence Durrell, *Justine* (New York: E. P. Dutton, 1957), 252.

25. J. R. R. Tolkien, *The Fellowship of the Ring, Being the First Part of The Lord of the Rings*, 2d ed. (Boston: Houghton Mifflin, 1965), 60.

26. Tolkien, *The Fellowship of the Ring,* 65.

27. MIT computer scientist Richard Stallman launched the open-source movement in 1984 when he devised a legal device called the General Public License (GPL) or "copyleft." Anything licensed under a copyleft is in the public domain, as are all derivative products that use any portion of the copylefted code. A typical "copyleft" notice reads as follows: "The information in this article is free. It may be copied, distributed, and/or modified under the conditions set down in the Design Science License published by Michael Stutz at dsl.org/copyleft/dsl.txt. Accessed 1 June 2002.

28. Osama bin Laden was the only sibling in the large bin Laden family who never studied abroad, according to Allen E. Goodman, "International Education: Does America Need Another Book by Henry Kissinger," *Vital Speeches* 68 (15 October 2001): 28.   To read more about the views of Osama bin Laden, see www.pbs.org/wgbh/pages/frontline/shows/binladen. Accessed 27 May 2002.

29. Islam itself claims 2 billion adherents worldwide.

30. This evangelistic strategy seems to be working. Muslim clerics say that the number of conversions to Islam has quadrupled since Nine-Eleven. See "America the Sensible," *The Economist* 27 (October 2001): 34.

31. At the time of this writing, IBM's reemergence as a force to be reckoned with is being powered by open-standards technologies, which are stitching together diverse hardware and software systems.

32. Eric S. Raymond, *The Cathedral and the Bazaar: Musings on Linux and Open Source by an Accidental Revolutionary*, rev. ed. (Cambridge, MA: O'Reilly, 2001), 21.

33. Netcraft surveys millions of websites worldwide each month to see what operating systems and Web servers they're running. As of December 2001, Apache is running on 63% of websites worldwide, more than twice as many as Microsoft and 30 times as many as Sun iPlanet. Linux is running on 30% of those sites, three times Solaris and catching up to Microsoft. In 2001, Linux grew at 24%. For the most recent statistics, see www.netcraft.com/Survey/. Accessed 2 May 2002. Go to Google, use Linux to do the search, and find the site "Companies Using Linux."

34. See "OpenCola Softdrink version 1.1.3," www.colawp.com/colas/400/cola467–recipe.html. Accessed 11 February 2003.

35. Http://eon.law.harvard.edu/openlaw/. Accessed 1 June 2002.

36. www.openmusicregistry.org. Accessed 1 June 2002.

37. www.wikipedia.com. Accessed 1 June 2002. This is a copylefted, web-based encyclopedia that in one year collected more than 26,000 articles.

38. Here's an example of an open-source spirituality. Actress Penelope Cruz professes, "I was baptized and had my first communion, and I believe in God in my own ways. But the

philosophy I most identify with is Buddhism because it's the one that doesn't say, 'This is the only way.' I don't want to put a title on what I believe." As quoted in "Overheard," *Plugged In* (May 2001): 10. For more, see Nathan Brockman, "Yes, Virginia, You Are an Open-Source Theologian, A Hacker of Your Soul. Here's the Manual. Then Get Thee on-Line," *Spirituality and Health* (Winter 2002): 54–55. www.spiritualityhealth.com/newsh/items/article/item_4009.html.

39. Brian Pierse has made the interesting observation that while most saints get their own feast days, since ancient times the church has made its two great pillars Peter and Paul share the same feast day. For more, see Brian Pierse, "Peter *And* Paul: Not 'Either/Or' But 'Both/And,'"*Spirituality* (May-June 2002): 143–49.

40. For more on the "open" person, see Wolfhart Pannenberg, *Anthropology in Theological Perspective*, trans. M. O'Connell (Philadelphia: Westminster Press, 1985), 71–79.

41. Companies that now "double-boot," using Linux as well as Microsoft, include Google, eBay, Akamai, Netscape, Amazon, and IBM. Even Microsoft now has an informal partnership with Linux called "Mono" ("monkey" in Spanish) that will produce a free edition of Microsoft's ".Net," which Microsoft hopes will become the common language for next-generation computing.

42. Philippians 3:13.

43. See Acts 2:14–40.

44. I do think that historians will date the beginning of the 21st century at 8:45 A.M. on 11 September 2001. See William E. Hull, "Religion and the World Crisis," *Christian Ethics Today* (December 2001): 6–10. www.christianethicstoday.com/Issue/037/...htm. Accessed 7 June 2002.

45. Mike Ball writes, "This year alone the world will generate over two gigabytes of information for every human being on the planet. . . . Statistically, human beings can read and process approximately 4 gigabytes of information in their lifetimes. This certainly makes for an interesting dilemma since the hard drive on a personal computer can contain 16 gigabytes of information, or 4 times more than you can effectively use in your lifetime!" (Mike Ball, "Welcome to the Knowledge Age," *Transform Magazine* [December 2001]: 7).

www.transformmag.com/db_area/archs/2001/12/whitepapers/ wpser.shtml. Accessed 1 June 2002.

46. Mark C. Taylor, *The Moment of Complexity: Emerging Network Culture* (Chicago: University of Chicago Press, 2001), 3.

47. William Van Dusen Wishard, "Between Two Ages: Get Used to It," *Vital Speeches of the Day* 68 (15 January 2002): 207.

48. Bill Joy, "Why the Future Doesn't Need Us," *Wired* (April 2000), 239–62. www.wired.com/wired/archive/8.04/joy.html. Accessed 11 February 2003.

49. Tim Lambon, "Letter from Jabal Saraj" reporting on the coverage of the war in Afghanistan in *TLS: Times Literary Supplement,* 19 October 2001, 15.

50. Jürgen Moltmann, *A Theology of Hope* (New York: Harper & Row, 1967), 16.

51. Paul J. Achtemeier, *Romans*, Interpretation: A Bible Commentary for Teaching and Preaching (Atlanta: John Knox Press, 1985), 212.

52. Luke 4:18–19.

53. Winston Churchill, as quoted at the end of A. G. Hopkins's foreword to *Globalization in World History,* ed. A. G. Hopkins (New York: W. W. Norton, 2002).

54. See the fascinating account of the treatment of Methodists: "Madness in Their Methodism: Religious Enthusiasm, the Mad-Doctors, and the Case of Alexander Cruden," in Jonathan Andrews and Andrew Scull, *Undertaker of the Mind: John Monro and Mad-Doctoring in Eighteenth-Century England* (Berkeley: University of California Press, 2002), 73–116.

55. As quoted in Elise Schellenberg, "Chinese Christians Pay Ultimate Price," Christianity.ca (Evangelical Fellowship of Canada), 16 January 2002. www.christianity.ca/missions/persecuted_stories/chinese_christ ians_pay_price.php. Accessed 11 February 2003.

56. The Bowers were sent by the Association of Baptists for World Evangelism, based in New Cumberland, PA. Husband Jim, 38, and their son Cory, six, lived. See "From Peru: ABWE, The Bowers, and an International Tragedy," www.backtothebible.org/new/bowers_abwe.html. Accessed 27 May 2002.

57. David Rohde, "A Nation Challenged: Al Qaeda: Verses From bin Laden's War: Wielding the Pen as a Sword of the Jihad," *New York Times*, 7 April 2002, 20.

58. See, for example, Kim Stanley Robinson, *The Years of Rice and Salt* (New York: Bantam Books, 2002).

59. Pascal Boyer, *Religion Explained: The Evolutionary Origins of Religious Thought* (New York: Basic Books, 2002), 262.

60. The scholar continues, "Yet religious feeling has not died. It has rather gone underground. It preserves its 'secret life' in comics, cartoons and science-fiction films, where it has undergone a characteristic transformation. In Freudian terms, it has been repressed and thereby perverted. The supernatural has become the grotesque: 'lacking an allowable connection with the transcendent, we have substituted an obsessive, unconscious focus on the negative dimension of the experience'" (Edward Skidelsky, "The Spirit Thing," [Review of Victoria Nelson, *The Secret Life of Puppets*], *TLS: Times Literary Supplement*, 25 January 2002, 7).

61. As quoted in Skidelsky, "The Spirit Thing," 7. Victoria Nelson, *The Secret Life of Puppets* (Cambridge, MA: Harvard University Press, 2001), explores the implication of this fact for popular culture.

62. Benjamin Cheever, "Judge Not," in Rick Moody and Darcey Steinke, *Joyful Noise: The New Testament Revisited* (Boston: Little, Brown, 1997), 172.

63. Andy Butcher, "America Losing Its Christian Faith—But Finding Others," *Charisma News Service Online*, 28 December 2001. www.charismanews.com/online/articledisplay.pl?ArticleID=16272. Accessed 5 May 2002.

64. Philip Jenkins, *The Next Christendom: The Coming of Global Christianity* (New York: Oxford University Press, 2002), 216.

65. Wishard, "Between Two Ages: Get Used to It," 208.

66. "But not all the Christian imagery was omitted; an elongated Last Supper table, the chorus ranged in a row behind it, stretched the width of the Covent Garden stage" (Andrew Porter, "Invisible Thoughts," *TLS: Times Literary Supplement*, 21 December 2001, 17).

67. Anthony Alofsin, "Brother Philippe's Air: The Day the Museum Finally Became Our Church," *TLS: Times Literary Supplement*, 21 December 2001, 12.

68. As quoted in Alofsin, "Brother Philippe's Air," 12.

69. Kenneth L. Woodward, "The Changing Face of the Church," *Newsweek*, 16 April 2001, 48.

70. Jenkins, *The Next Christendom*, 77.

71. Second Timothy 3:5 (NIV) talks about churches "having a form of godliness but denying its power." But the author immediately issues this warning about such churches: "Have nothing to do with them."

72. This is the backdrop to Andrew Chesnut's quip about "third world Christianity," where "The Catholic Church has chosen the poor, but the poor chose the Pentecostals." As quoted by Jenkins, *The Next Christendom*, 156.

73. Roy Fuller, "Buried Treasure," in his *Available for Dreams* (London: Collins Harvill, 1989), 112.

74. Hebrews 1:1 NIV.

75. St. Augustine, *De Baptismo Contra Donatistas*, V, c.xxvii, n.38 (PL, xliii, 196).

76. See Gerald McDermott, *Can Evangelicals Learn from World Religions: Jesus, Revelation and Religious Traditions* (Downers Grove, IL: InterVarsity Press, 2000).

77. John Calvin, *Institutes of the Christian Religion*, trans. Henry Beveridge (Grand Rapids: Eerdmans, 1964), 1:236.

78. As quoted in Makato Fujimura, "Form *and* Content: That Final Dance" in *It was Good: Making Art to the Glory of God*, ed. Ned Bustard (Baltimore, MD: Square Halo Books, 2000), 58.

79. Charlene Spretnak, *States of Grace: The Recovery of Meaning in the Postmodern Age* (San Francisco: HarperSanFrancisco, 1991), 90.

80. "Responses to the *Lineamenta*," *East Asian Pastoral Review* (Manila) 35, no. 1 (1998): 75.

81. This is the compelling argument of Jenkins, *The Next Christendom*.

82. I borrow this phrase "cultural circumcision" from Hans Jochum Margull in an article for *Christian Comment* 53, as quoted in Mark Gibbs and T. Ralph Morton, *God's Lively People* (Philadelphia: Westminster Press, 1971), 194.

83. There is a lot of spiritual cross-dressing going on: the liberals being most opposed to the "thereness" and the conservatives most willing to embrace the "theres."

84. Arthur M. Schlesinger, *The Cycles of American History* (Boston: Houghton Mifflin, 1986), xi.

85. "The So-Called Letter to Diognetus," in *Early Christian Fathers*, ed. Cyril C. Richardson (Philadelphia, PA: Westminster Press, 1953), 216.

86. See especially the work of David Korten, *The Post-Corporate World: Life after Capitalism* (San Francisco: Barrett-Koehler, 1999), and *When Corporations Rule the World*, 2d ed. (San Francisco: Barrett-Koehler, 2001).

87. Brian O'Keefe, "Global Brands: Tricon, the Company that Owns Both KFC and Pizza Hut," *Fortune*, 26 November 2001, 104. www.fortune.com/. Accessed 7 June 2002.

88. Both Egypt and Saudi Arabia are trying to get *more* McDonald's franchises.

89. Henry Fielding, *The History of Tom Jones: A Foundling* (New York: Random House, 1964), 69.

90. Warren I. Cohen, *The Asian American Century* (Cambridge, MA: Harvard University Press, 2002), 79–127.

91. Diana L. Eck, *A New Religious America: How a "Christian Country" Has Now Become the World's Most Religiously Diverse Nation* (San Francisco: HarperSanFrancisco, 2001), 1.

92. Notice that the both-and nature of multicultural and global are revealed in one study, which showed that 98% of Latino parents in Miami felt it was imperative for their children to become competent in English. By contrast, only 94% of Anglo parents felt the same about English. See the Rand Corporation study, as analyzed in sociologist Vincent N. Parillo, "A Challenge for Educators," *Vital Speeches of the Day* 68 (15 October 2001): 23.

93. My favorite name for a church is Mosaic (Los Angeles), where Erwin McManus is pastor. Up to 50 nations come together at Mosaic, and McManus works the image of broken and fragmented people brought together by a master craftsman. The cracks, of course, are where the light shines through most brilliantly.

94. As quoted in Robert G. Tuttle Jr., *Can We Talk? Sharing Your Faith in a Pre-Christian World* (Nashville: Abingdon Press, 1999), 51.

95. Acts 6:14 NIV.

96. Caryl Phillips, *A New World Order: Selected Essays* (London: Secker and Warburg, 2001).

97. Richard Pipes, *Communism: A Brief History* (New York: Modern Library, 2001), 158.

98. Charles Paul Freund, "2001 Nights: The End of the Orientalist Critique," *Reason* (December 2001): 63–70.

99. As quoted in "Trade in Rare Gems Aids al Qaeda," *Wall Street Journal*, 16 November 2001, A8.

100. Doris Lessing, *The Sweetest Dream* (New York: HarperCollins, 2001).

101. Andrew McMurry writes, "We can no less do without the concept of 'truth' than we can do without gravity; that we cannot actually grasp either does not mean we can ignore them, for we rely on their effects to organize our actions. You do not have to believe in 'gravity' to live, but to live you must understand 'falling'" (Andrew McMurry, "The Possibility of Literary Meaning: A Peircean Suggestion for Derrida and Rorty," *Soundings* 79 [1996]: 485–86).

102. Tommy Shaw and James Young, "Brave New World," *Unofficial Styx Lyrics Archive*, www.styxnet.com/styxlyrics/bnw2.htm. Accessed 2 November 2001.

103. John 20:21 NIV.

104. With thanks to Steve Sallee, senior pastor of Cokesbury United Methodist Church, Knoxville, Tennessee, for this modulation of "be there" to "I'm in."

105. Martin Buber, *Moses: The Revelation and the Covenant* (New York: Harper Torchbooks, 1958). See his explanation on pages 51–53. I want to thank Dr. James Moore, St. Luke's United Methodist Church in Houston for first pointing out Buber's position.

106. Martin Buber, *Moses* (Oxford: East & West Library, 1946), 51–53.

107. Psalm 139:7–10.

108. "Ghost of Tom Joad," in Rage Against the Machine (musical group), *Renegades*, audio CD, New York: Epic, 2000. See also Rage Against the Machine, "The Ghost of Tom Joad," http://banners.pennyweb.com/tcexit/exit.html. Accessed 12 February 2003.

Chapter Three

1. These sentiments, verified by John Drane via e-mail, are expanded in his *Cultural Change and Biblical Faith: The Future of the Church: Biblical and Missiological Essays for the New Century* (Waynesboro, GA: Paternoster, 2000), and his *The McDonaldization of the Church: Consumer Culture and the Church's Future* (Macon, GA: Smyth & Helwys, 2002).

2. See John H. Piet, "Two Ways of Doing Theology," *Perspectives* 6 (September 1991): 16–18.

3. Australian theologians Michael Frost and Alan Hirsch define Christendom thinking as "attractional, dualistic and hierarchical" rather than a missional mindset of "incarnational, messianic, and apostolic." See their wonderful book *The Shaping of Things to Come: Innovation and Mission for the 21st-Century Church* (Peabody, MA: Hendrickson Publishers, 2003).

4. Quoted in Polly LaBarre, "After Shock," *Fast Company* (January 2002): 29.

5. See Luke 10:27.

6. As quoted in Elisabeth Elliot, *Through Gates of Splendor* (New York: Harper & Row, 1957), 20.

7. *Ecstatic Confessions*, collected and introduced by Martin Buber, ed. Paul Mendes-Flohr, trans. Esther Cameron (San Francisco: Harper & Row, 1985), 18–19.

8. As quoted in Frederic Raphael, "Make Them Pop Like Chestnuts: The Dying Art of Being Quotable," *TLS: Times Literary Supplement*, 4 February 2000, 5.

9. Mark 3:14 NIV.

10. Luke 17:20 NIV.

11. John Shea, *The Spirit Master* (Chicago: Thomas More, 1987), 132.

12. Shea, *The Spirit Master,* 132–35.

13. For a more detailed treatment of the "with-me" principle, as first introduced by Richard Halverson, see E. Stanley Ott, *The Joy of Discipling: Friend with Friend, Heart with Heart* (Grand Rapids: Zondervan, 1989), especially 41–49.

14. Paul Welter is a former professor at Kearney State University in Nebraska. See his *How to Help a Friend* (Wheaton, IL: Tyndale House, 1978), 16–17. With thanks to Rhonda for pointing me to this resource.

15. Jeremiah 30:21 NIV.

16. Paul S. Fiddes moves us from the "observational" approach to the Trinity toward a "participational" understanding of the Trinity that takes relationships seriously. See his *Participating in God: A Pastoral Doctrine of the Trinity* (Louisville: Westminster John Knox Press, 2000), 55, 50.

17. Arthur C. McGill, *Death and Life: An American Theology* (Philadelphia: Fortress Press, 1987), 78.

18. McGill, *Death and Life,* 78.
19. Quoted in J. Philip Newell, *Echo of the Soul: The Sacredness of the Human Body* (Harrisburg, PA: Morehouse Publishing, 2000), 126. On the same page Newell writes, "It is not that God enters communion but that God is communion."
20. 1 John 4:8.
21. Naguib Mahfouz, *Echoes of an Autobiography*, trans. Denys Johnson-Davies (New York: Doubleday, 1997), 107.
22. Robert Browning, "Fra Lippo Lippi," in *The Poems and Plays of Robert Browning* (New York: Modern Library, 1934), 210.
23. H. Schmidt, "The Strange Properties of Psychokinesis," *Journal of Scientific Exploration* 1 (1987): 103–18.
24. R. Targ and H. E. Puthoff, "Information Transmission Under Conditions of Sensory Shielding," *Nature* 251 (1974): 602–7.
25. Dean I. Radin, *The Conscious Universe: The Scientific Truth of Psychic Phenomena* (New York: HarperEdge, 1997); E. C. May et al., "Review of the Psychoenergetic Research Conducted at SRI International (1973–1988)," *SRI International Technical Report* (March 1988).
26. R. C. Byrd, "Positive Therapeutic Effects of Intercessory Prayer in a Coronary Care Unit Population," *Southern Medical Journal* 81 (1988): 826–29.
27. Abraham H. Maslow, "Religious Aspects of Peak-Experience," in his *Religions, Values, and Peak Experiences* (New York: Viking Press, 1970), Appendix A, 59-68.
28. Jim Forest, *Praying with Icons* (Maryknoll, NY: Orbis Books, 1997), 83–84.
29. McGill, *Death and Life,* 61.
30. Hillel Schwartz, *The Culture of the Copy: Striking Likenesses, Unreasonable Facsimiles* (New York: Zone Books, 1996), 381.
31. 1 Corinthians 4:7 RSV. See McGill, *Death and Life,* 64.
32. W. H. Auden, *Lectures on Shakespeare*, ed. Arthur Kirsch (Princeton, NJ: Princeton University Press, 2000), 273.
33. As quoted in Andrew Boyd, *Daily Afflictions: The Agony of Being Connected to Everything in the Universe* (New York: W. W. Norton, 2002), 16.
34. Romans 12:5 NIV, emphasis mine.
35. Sobonfu Somé, *The Spirit of Intimacy: Ancient African Teachings in the Ways of Relationships* (New York: William Morrow, 1999), 34.
36. Somé, *The Spirit of Intimacy,* 117.

37. Somé, *The Spirit of Intimacy,* 75.

38. Bryan Dyson, in a speech delivered to Coca-Cola, as transcribed in Matt Church Seminars, "The Chemistry of Success Articles: The Present," www.mattchurch.com.au/articles.html or www.eservice.com.au/cgi-bin/cgiwrap/eservice/allegro.pl? database.matt.articles.item36. Accessed 26 January 2002.

39. Pamela Paul, "Millennial Myths," *American Demographics* 23 (December 2001): 20.

40. David Whyte, *Crossing the Unknown Sea: Work as a Pilgrimage of Identity* (New York: Riverhead Books, 2001), 178.

41. In words that demonstrate clever theological machismo, Marx wrote, "The science of *wealth* is therefore simultaneously the science of renunciation. . . . The less you eat, drink and buy books; the less you go to the theater, the dance hall, the public house; the less you think, love, theorize, sing, paint, fence, etc., the more you save—the *greater* becomes your treasure which neither moths nor rust will devour—your *capital.* The less you *are,* the less you express your own life, the more you *have"* (Karl Marx, *Economic and Philosophic Manuscripts of 1844* [Moscow: Progress Publishers, 1974], 104).

42. As found in letter 193: "To Samuel Bowles, late August 1858?" in *The Letters of Emily Dickinson,* ed. Thomas H. Johnson (Cambridge, MA: Belknap Press of Harvard University Press, 1958), 2:338.

43. Martha Simmons and Frank A. Thomas, "Ubuntu," *African American Pulpit* 4 (Fall 2001): 6. See also Archbishop Desmond Tutu's definition of this in Zia Jaffrey, "The Travails of Desmond Tutu: An Interview with a Historic Figure in South Africa's Freedom Struggle," *Daily Camera* (Boulder, CO), 1 March 1998.

44. Alex Boraine, *A Country Unmasked* (New York: Oxford University Press, 2000), 362.

45. See Galatians 6:2.

46. With thanks to Steve Redmond for this insight.

47. Gideon Byamugisha, "Afterword," in Gideon Mendel, *A Broken Landscape: HIV and AIDS in Africa* (London: Network Photographers in Association with Actionaid, 2001), 199.

48. As quoted in *Movies,* ed. Gilbert Adair (New York: Penguin Books, 1999), 355.

49. In the American Revolution, field hospitals were butchers' tents where, according to one eyewitness, "the sick were attended by the sick, the dying by the dying." Quoted in John Cannon, "To Battle in a Top Hat," *TLS: Times Literary Supplement*, 18 January 2002, 39. See also Richard Holmes, *Redcoat: The British Soldier in the Age of Horse and Musket* (London: HarperCollins, 2002).

50. Oscar Wilde said of George Bernard Shaw that "he hasn't an enemy in the world and none of his friends like him." One wonders if NUTS disciples aren't exactly the opposite? Plenty of people will hate us and disagree with us. But authenticity and honesty will prevail so that our worst enemies can't help but admire and respect who we are.

51. Don DeLillo, *Underworld* (New York: Scribner, 1997), 51.

52. Helen H. Lemmel, "Turn Your Eyes upon Jesus," as found in *The United Methodist Hymnal: Book of United Methodist Worship* (Nashville: The United Methodist Publishing House, 1989), 349.

53. With thanks to colleague Daren I. Flinck for this insight.

54. Peter Weiss, "The Brazil Nut Effect Gets More Jumbled," *Science News* 160 (17 November 2001): 309.

55. As quoted in Elysa Gardner, "Honorees Rock to a Different Drummer," *USA Today*, 21 March 2001, 4D.

56. Joseph P. Shapiro and Andrea R. Wright, "Can Churches Save America?" *U. S. News & World Report*, 9 September 1996, 46–53.

57. According to a 2001 Barna Research Group poll commissioned by World Vision. "Only 3 percent of evangelicals say they plan to help with AIDS internationally, compared with 8 percent of non-Christians. . . . Evangelicals were also the least likely to support children orphaned by AIDS." See Sheryl Henderson Blunt, "Bono Tells Christians: Don't Neglect Africa," *Christianity Today,* 22 April 2002, 18. christianitytoday.com/ct/2002/005/14.18.html. Accessed 4 June 2002.

58. Ted Haggard, *Dog Training, Fly Fishing and Sharing Christ in the 21st Century* (Nashville: Thomas Nelson, 2002).

59. As quoted in *Fortune*, 26 November 2001, 108.

60. "Terrorism Is Not the Only Scourge" and "International Aid: The Health of Nations," *Economist*, 22 December 2001–4 January 2002, 10, 83.

61. *The Letters of Pelagius and His Followers,* ed. B. R. Reese (Rochester, NY: Boydell, 1991), 75.
62. See Luke 16:19–31.
63. See Matthew 25:42–43.
64. William Raspberry, "When Social Conscience Gives Way to Despair," *Chicago Tribune,* 9 September 1991, 15.

Chapter Four

1. The opening words of chapter 22 of Herman Melville, *Billy Budd, Sailor: An Inside Narrative,* ed. Milton R. Stern (Indianapolis: Bobbs-Merrill, 1975), 97.
2. So states Genesis 9:8–17.
3. To the ancient Greeks the appearance of the rainbow was a manifestation of Iris, who brought messages from the gods of danger and retribution. The bow of peace could easily become the bow of war, as in Egyptian antiquity, or the rainbow serpent or python, as in the aboriginal cultures of Australia, Papua New Guinea, and the Semang of Malaysia. The Zulus feared the rainbow—which they believed brought pestilence and could enter the body and make it sick.
4. Williams says, "Somewhere between my fun-loving but apparently self-involved mother, who was a Christian Scientist and thought everything was wonderful, and my frequently absent, remote industrialist father, who was a pragmatist and thought, 'everybody's out to nail ya' . . . My comedy steers between rainbows and cesspools" (Robin Williams in *The New Yorker,* 8 April 2002, as quoted in Dick Staub's *CultureWatch,* April 2002, 3).
5. Ecclesiastes 7:15 NIV.
6. Psalm 73:12-13 NIV.
7. Job 21:7 NIV.
8. John 16:33 NASB.
9. Matthew 27:46.
10. The young girl, Judith, is reflecting on the day Jacob, her teenage brother, was accused of a brutal murder. The ensuing ordeal threatened to destroy the family. Life as they knew it was gone forever. "Before" and "after" became the chasm that ensnared the family despair, deceit, and distrust.
11. Alice Hoffman, *At Risk* (New York: Putnam's, 1988), 37.

12. *The Notebooks and Papers of Gerard Manley Hopkins*, ed. Humphry House (New York: Oxford University Press, 1937), 342.
13. W. B. Yeats, "Easter 1916," in his *The Poems*, 2d ed., ed. Richard J. Finneran (New York: Scribner, 1997), 184.
14. "Content with whatever I have" (Philippians 4:11).
15. Philippians 4:13.
16. Mark 10:27.
17. 1 Corinthians 3:21.
18. Ephesians 3:20 KJV.
19. Philippians 4:19 KJV.
20. The refrain of the hymn "I Hear the Savior Say," written by Elvina M. Hall in 1868.
21. This image of the Word of God as a pacemaker comes from George Steiner.
22. In order, Revelation 21:4, 5, 7 KJV; Ephesians 6:16; 1 John 1:7, 9 NRSV; and Ephesians 6:21 KJV.
23. Colossians 3:11.
24. 1 Corinthians 15:28.
25. Genesis 28:15–16.
26. Philippians 3:8 KJV.
27. Luke 10:27.
28. 1 Corinthians 9:21 RSV and Galatians 6:2 RSV and NRSV.
29. Denis Devlin, "The Colors of Love," in his *Selected Poems* (New York: Holt, Rinehart and Winston, 1963), 54.
30. John 15:12.
31. 2 Corinthians 1:3 NIV.
32. 1 Corinthians 13:7.
33. These words come from Bishop John A. T. Robinson's valedictory sermon as he was about to die from cancer. John A. T. Robinson, "Learning from Cancer," in his *Where Three Ways Meet* (London: SCM Press, 1987), 189.
34. Wisdom of Solomon 12:1.
35. Jeremiah 33:3 NASB.
36. Romans 11:36.
37. Colossians 1:17, 19–20.
38. 1 Timothy 6:19 NIV.
39. Ian McEwan's novel called *Enduring Love* (New York: Anchor Books, 1997) plays on the pun of its title.
40. William Shakespeare, Sonnet 116.
41. 2 Corinthians 4:16 Living Bible.

42. One of the best descriptions of "crazy love" is found in 1 Corinthians 13.

43. Mark 3:21.

44. Paraphrase of Acts 26:24–25.

45. 2 Corinthians 5:13, as quoted in Wick Broomall, "The Second Epistle to the Corinthians," in *The Wycliffe Bible Commentary,* ed. Charles F. Pfeiffer and Everett F. Harrison (Chicago: Moody Press, 1962), 1271.   I want to thank Erwin McManus for reminding me of one of his favorite verses of Scripture.

46. Thus R. A. Knox paraphrases: "I expect you to think I must be mad, going on talking about myself like this; if so, treat it as an aside only meant for God; but if you can see sense in it it is meant for you." For a critique of this approach, see R. V. G. Tasker, *The Second Epistle of Paul to the Corinthians*, Tyndale New Testament Commentaries (London: Tyndale, 1958), 85.

47. "The total understanding of this passage may be beyond our grasp" (Ralph P. Martin, *2 Corinthians,* Word Biblical Commentary 40 [Waco, TX: Word Books, 1986], 126).

48. Wick Broomall, "The Second Epistle to the Corinthians," in *The Wycliffe Bible Commentary*, ed. Charles F. Pfeiffer and Everett F. Harrison (Chicago: Moody Press, 1962), 1271.

49. Romans 12:3.

50. It is true that Paul does not use *mania* ("insanity") or *mainomai* ("to be insane"), words he used before Festus (Acts 26:24–25) to describe his "madness."

51. Caroline Moosehead, "How the Troublemakers Shamed the Abusers," *TLS: Times Literary Supplement*, 7 September 2001, 27.

52. Jonathan Power, *Like Water on Stone: The Story of Amnesty International* (Boston: Northeastern University Press, 2001), xi, 119–22.

53. 1 Peter 5:7.

54. Ephesians 6:18 NIV.

55. Philippians 4:7.

56. See Galatians 2:20; Romans 14:7–9.

57. As quoted in Andrew Boyd, *Daily Afflictions: The Agony of Being Connected to Everything in the Universe* (New York: W. W. Norton, 2002), 20.

58. Anna B. Warner, 1860s.

59. Robert Lowry, "Nothing but the Blood," 1876.

60. Lela B. Long, 20th century.

61. William J. and Gloria Gaither, 1971.
62. Civilla D. Martin, "God Will Take Care of You," 1904.
63. Andraé Crouch, 1978.
64. Lanny Wolfe, 1977.
65. Edward Mote, "The Solid Rock," 1834.
66. Charlotte Elliott, " Just As I Am, Without One Plea," 1822.
67. Mary A. Lathbury, "Break Thou the Bread of Life," 1877.

Index

Do You Know the Postmodern Alphabet?

A Is for Abductive
The Language of the Emerging Church

Leonard Sweet, Brian D. McLaren,
and Jerry Haselmayer

The letters are all the same, but the things they stand for are as different as the future is from the past. *A Is for Abductive* helps you get a handle today on the vocabulary of tomorrow, and on concepts indispensable for living out the old-fashioned gospel in these newfangled times.

"You caused this book," writes one of the authors. "People like you were insisting on a beginner's guide to the pathway of postmodern ministry." Here it is. There is no right or wrong place to begin—just pick a letter and start reading. You'll acquire new words for a new world that will change how you think about church, about ministry, and about what it means to follow in Jesus' footsteps—entering today's culture in order to love it, serve it, and lead it home to God.

Softcover: 0-310-24356-4

Pick up a copy today at your favorite bookstore!

ZONDERVAN™

GRAND RAPIDS, MICHIGAN 49530 USA

WWW.ZONDERVAN.COM

SoulTsunami
Sink or Swim in New Millennium Culture
10 life rings for you and your church

Leonard Sweet

SoulTsunami is a fascinating look at the implications of our changing world for the church in the 21st century. With uncanny wisdom and trademark wit, Leonard Sweet explores ten key "futuribles" (precision guesses that fall short of predictions), expanding on and relating topics ranging from the reentry of theism and spiritual longing in contemporary society, to the impact of modern technology, the global renaissance, and models for the church to reach people caught in the cultural maelstrom. Here are eye-opening perspectives on the church from within and from without—from its surrounding society.

Lively, well-written, and provocative, *SoulTsunami* is a clarion call for Christians to remove their tunnel-vision glasses and take a good look at the swelling postmodern flood. It is also a voice of encouragement, affirming the church in its role as God's lifeboat. And it is a passionate, prophetic guide, pointing the way to reach a world swept out to sea.

Softcover: 0-310-24312-2
Abridged Audio Pages® Cassette: 0-310-22712-7

Pick up a copy today at your favorite bookstore!

GRAND RAPIDS, MICHIGAN 49530 USA

WWW.ZONDERVAN.COM

The Message Never Changes,
But Our Methods Must.

Carpe Mañana
Is Your Church Ready to Seize Tomorrow?

Leonard Sweet

If God so loved the world . . . then we
ought to, too. But how? While the
church dreams of old wineskins, the
future is arriving, and the world
around us has undergone a radical transformation. Those of us over
thirty are no longer natives of a modern culture, but immigrants in
a postmodern society that speaks the language of cyberspace, grap-
ples with the implications of robotics, nanotechnology, and bio-
engineering, and looks everywhere but to the church for spiritual
and moral guidance.

Yet the gospel sun, far from setting, is poised to shine on this new
frontier—provided we'll seize tomorrow and its unprecedented
opportunities. The possibilities are limitless for those of us who
choose to live as Jesus lived, as people of our time and culture.
Carpe Mañana helps us go native. In nine "naturalization classes,"
Leonard Sweet speeds us toward influence in this postmodern
world—a world hungry to encounter the God who knows its soul,
speaks its language, and loves it with an all-transforming love.

Hardcover: 0-310-23947-8
Softcover: 0-310-25012-9

Pick up a copy today at your favorite bookstore!

ZONDERVAN™

GRAND RAPIDS, MICHIGAN 49530 USA

WWW.ZONDERVAN.COM